Guest-edited by
Owen Hopkins

MULTISPACE

ARCHITECTURE AT THE DAWN OF THE METAVERSE

06 | Vol 93 | 2023

MULTISPACE: ARCHITECTURE
AT THE DAWN OF THE METAVERSE

06/2023

About the Guest-editor 5

Owen Hopkins

Introduction 6

Architects in Multispace

Owen Hopkins

The Portal Galleries 14

Researching Portals in Fiction from the 19th Century to the Present

Lara Lesmes and Fredrik Hellberg

The Home as an Infinite Screen 22

Lucia Tahan

Hidden Infrastructures 30

From 'Spy-Hubs' to Hollow Buildings that Conceal the New Digital

Wendy W Fok

Architecture in Postreality 38

Emerging Approaches to Space in Hybrid Realities

Jesse Damiani

Touching, Licking, Tasting 48

Performing Multisensory Spatial Perception Through Extended-Reality Models

Paula Strunden

Multipurpose Domesticity 56

Labour, Leisure and Kitchen Tables

Holly Nielsen

Conjunctions 64

Or, Space as Oxymoron

Giacomo Pala

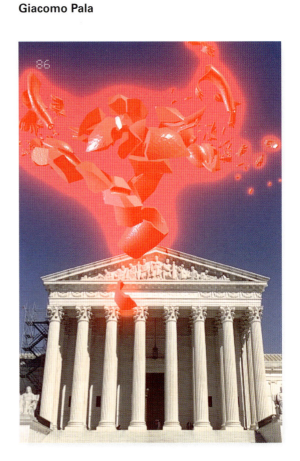

ISSN 0003-8504 ISBN 978 1 394 16354 0   Guest-edited by **Owen Hopkins**

Celebrating the Glitch — 72
The Multispatial Work of Ibiye Camp

Owen Hopkins

Architecture is Interface — 78
Latent Virtuality from Antiquity to Zoom

Joshua Bard and Francesca Torello

Very Big Art — 86
Follies, the Public and Multispace

Andrew Kovacs

Ways of Worlding — 94
Building Alternative Futures in Multispace

Alice Bucknell

The Anti-Metaverse — 104
Multispace and the Intersections of Reality

Micaela Mantegna and Marcelo Rinesi

All At Once – From Zoom Fatigue to Immersive Digital Experiences — 112
Why Architecture Must Adapt

Sasha Belitskaja

Shifting Contexts — 122
Liam Young's Prototypes of Architectural Futures

Owen Hopkins

> 'In multispace we are both the truest expression of ourselves and a single point in an incomprehensibly large and constantly growing dataset'
> — Owen Hopkins

From Another Perspective

The Haçienda Must Be Built — 128

Neil Spiller

Contributors — 134

Editorial Offices
John Wiley & Sons
9600 Garsington Road
Oxford
OX4 2DQ

T +44 (0)18 6577 6868

Editor
Neil Spiller

Managing Editor
Caroline Ellerby
Caroline Ellerby Publishing

Freelance Contributing Editor
Abigail Grater

Publisher
Todd Green

Art Direction + Design
Christian Küsters
CHK Design

Production Editor
Elizabeth Gongde

Prepress
Artmedia, London

Printed in the United Kingdom
by Hobbs the Printers Ltd

Front cover
Modified details of a still from Cao Fei (Second Life avatar: China Tracey), *RMB City: A Second Life City Planning*, 2007. Courtesy of the artist, Vitamin Creative Space and Sprüth Magers. Cover design by CHK Design

Inside front cover
untitled, xyz, *Monument of Errors*, 2022. © untitled, xyz

Page 1
Keiken, *Player of Cosmic ☽°Realms*, shown at 'WORLDBUILDING: Gaming and Art in the Digital Age', Julia Stoschek Collection, Düsseldorf, 2022. Courtesy of the artists and Julia Stoschek Collection

EDITORIAL BOARD

Denise Bratton
Paul Brislin
Mark Burry
Helen Castle
Nigel Coates
Peter Cook
Kate Goodwin
Edwin Heathcote
Brian McGrath
Jayne Merkel
Peter Murray
Mark Robbins
Deborah Saunt
Patrik Schumacher
Jill Stoner
Ken Yeang

ARCHITECTURAL DESIGN
November/December 2023
Volume 93
Issue 06

Disclaimer
The Publisher and Editors cannot be held responsible for errors or any consequences arising from the use of information contained in this journal; the views and opinions expressed do not necessarily reflect those of the Publisher and Editors, neither does the publication of advertisements constitute any endorsement by the Publisher and Editors of the products advertised.

Journal Customer Services
For ordering information, claims and any enquiry concerning your journal subscription please go to www.wileycustomerhelp.com/ask or contact your nearest office.

Americas
E: cs-journals@wiley.com
T: +1 877 762 2974

Europe, Middle East and Africa
E: cs-journals@wiley.com
T: +44 (0)1865 778 315

Asia Pacific
E: cs-journals@wiley.com
T: +65 6511 8000

Japan (for Japanese-speaking support)
E: cs-japan@wiley.com
T: +65 6511 8010

Visit our Online Customer Help available in 7 languages at www.wileycustomerhelp.com/ask

Print ISSN: 0003-8504
Online ISSN: 1554-2769

Prices are for six issues and include postage and handling charges. Individual-rate subscriptions must be paid by personal cheque or credit card. Individual-rate subscriptions may not be resold or used as library copies.

All prices are subject to change without notice.

Identification Statement
Periodicals Postage paid at Rahway, NJ 07065. Air freight and mailing in the USA by Mercury Media Processing, 1850 Elizabeth Avenue, Suite C, Rahway, NJ 07065, USA.

USA Postmaster
Please send address changes to *Architectural Design*, John Wiley & Sons Inc., c/o The Sheridan Press, PO Box 465, Hanover, PA 17331, USA

Rights and Permissions
Requests to the Publisher should be addressed to:
Permissions Department
John Wiley & Sons Ltd
The Atrium
Southern Gate
Chichester
West Sussex PO19 8SQ
UK

F: +44 (0)1243 770 620
E: Permissions@wiley.com

All Rights Reserved. No part of this publication may be reproduced, stored in a retrieval system or transmitted in any form or by any means, electronic, mechanical, photocopying, recording, scanning or otherwise, except under the terms of the Copyright, Designs and Patents Act 1988 or under the terms of a licence issued by the Copyright Licensing Agency Ltd, 5th Floor, Shackleton House, Battle Bridge Lane, London SE1 2HX, without the permission in writing of the Publisher.

Subscribe to ⌂
⌂ is published bimonthly and is available to purchase on both a subscription basis and as individual volumes at the following prices.

Prices
Individual copies:
£29.99 / US$45.00
Mailing fees for print may apply

Annual Subscription Rates
Student: £97 / US$151
print only
Personal: £151 / US$236
print only
Institutional: £357 / US$666
online only
Institutional: £373 / US$695
print only
Institutional: £401 / US$748
print and online

ABOUT THE
GUEST-EDITOR

OWEN HOPKINS

The metaverse is coming. It has become a cliché to describe the Covid-19 pandemic as having accelerated existing trends, yet in terms of its impact on the relationship between the physical and digital worlds, this has, nevertheless, very much been the case. In this regard, Multispace is a lockdown project in more than a few ways, emerging for, and shaped during, an undergraduate dissertation elective led by Owen Hopkins at Newcastle University across 2021 and 2022. Then as now, it is conceived as a conceptual/practical bulwark against the homogenising, commercialising and ultimately atomising forces driving the metaverse – open, inclusive and constantly in a state of transition.

Owen Hopkins is an architectural writer, historian and curator. He is Director of the Farrell Centre at Newcastle University, which opened in April 2023 as a vital new space for furthering public understanding of the critical roles of architecture and planning in shaping the contemporary world. He was previously Senior Curator of Exhibitions and Education at Sir John Soane's Museum in London, and before that Architecture Programme Curator at the city's Royal Academy of Arts. His work revolves around the connections between architecture, politics and society, the roles of style, media and technology in architectural discourse, and architecture's varying relationships to the public and popular culture. He is the curator of numerous exhibitions, including the Farrell Centre's inaugural exhibition, 'More with Less: Reimagining Architecture for a Changing World' (2023). At the Soane Museum, he curated the major exhibitions, 'Langlands & Bell: Degrees of Truth' (2020), 'Eric Parry: Drawing' (2019) and 'The Return of the Past: Postmodernism in British Architecture' (2018), as well as numerous small projects.

He is the author of eight books, including most recently *The Brutalists: Brutalism's Best Architects* (Phaidon, 2023), *The Museum: From its Origins to the 21st Century* (Frances Lincoln, 2021) and *Postmodern Architecture: Less is a Bore* (Phaidon, 2020). His monograph *From the Shadows: The Architecture and Afterlife of Nicholas Hawksmoor* (Reaktion, 2015) is a leading work on one of Britain's most significant architects. His first book, *Reading Architecture: A Visual Lexicon* (Laurence King, 2012), has been translated into 11 languages. He has also edited a further eight books, catalogues, journals and essay collections, including ⌂ *Multiform: Architecture in an Age of Transition* (January/February 2021), *Conversations on Postmodernism* (Sir John Soane's Museum, 2018) and *Sensing Architecture* (Royal Academy, 2017), and written over a hundred articles, opinion pieces and reviews for a range of publications.

A regular commentator in the national and international press, television and radio, Hopkins is regularly invited to give lectures at some of the world's most prestigious universities and cultural institutions, and is a frequent guest critic at architecture schools and a judge for various architecture awards. He is currently saving up for an Apple Vision Pro. ⌂

Text © 2023 John Wiley & Sons Ltd. Image © courtesy of Owen Hopkins

ARCHITECTS IN MULTISPACE

INTRODUCTION

OWEN HOPKINS

Adam Nathaniel Furman,
Queer de Triomf,
Barcelona Architecture Festival,
Barcelona,
2022

Multispace is queer space. Conceived as an exuberant and proud 'Arch of Alterity', Adam Nathaniel Furman's *Queer de Triomf* celebrates the LGBTQIA+ community's work in effecting a monumental shift in the acceptance of diverse gender expressions and sexual identities in Catalunya. Visible in AR on visitors' smartphones after scanning a QR code placed in front of the existing Arc de Triomf, the project illustrates multispace's possibilities of resisting single, determining narratives and creating spaces for multiplicity.

I think the potential of what the internet is going to do to society, both good and bad, is unimaginable. I think we're on the cusp of something exhilarating and terrifying ... It's an alien life-form ...

The breakthrough of the early part of the century with people like Duchamp who were so prescient ... The idea that the piece of work is not finished until the audience come to it and add their own interpretation. And what the piece of art is about is the grey space in the middle. That grey space in the middle is what the 21st century is going to be all about.

— David Bowie, 1999[1]

The history of the world is punctuated by people who have seemingly come from the future – or maybe from another world. Prophets, seers or prophesiers, these are people who can see the tectonic forces of history shifting and can detect their directions or trajectories and, in some instances, even their ultimate destinations. In articulating future conditions, experiences, identities and spaces, they anticipate more than they could possibly know. They imagine the unimaginable.

Just as Marcel Duchamp was a prophet for the 20th century, anticipating Pop Art, Conceptual Art and Postmodernism before the advent of Modernism, so David Bowie was/is a prophet for the 21st. Bowie both anticipated and prefigured today's simultaneous hyper-individualism and anonymisation, the consequent fragmentation of identity, and the erosion of the age-old distinctions between producer and consumer, between the creation of content and its consumption. And just as he foretold, the catalyst for these transformations has been the internet.

Where once the internet was something actively and consciously accessed – you sat down at a bulky desktop computer and 'dialled-up' – now it is ubiquitous; not just always on, but always there. Bowie's 'grey space in the middle' is not the internet itself, but the hybrid space its advent has created, the space that comes into being through the crossover between the physical and digital worlds. We call this multispace.

Back to the Beginning

Multispace exists in the intersection of the physical and digital and in the blurring of their previously clear dividing lines. Multispace is not a single space, but a hybrid space where we are, in effect, occupying multiple spaces simultaneously. It arises where the physical and digital intersect and collide. Multispace is the messy space in between, constantly in flux, its boundaries perpetually shifting. Multispace is both of the margins and of the centre. It is everywhere and nowhere. It is the new reality of the 21st century.

In multispace we are both the truest expression of ourselves and a single point in an incomprehensibly large and constantly growing dataset. In this way, multispace is both a reflection of, and plays its own part in, destabilising binaries that have defined the (Western) world since the

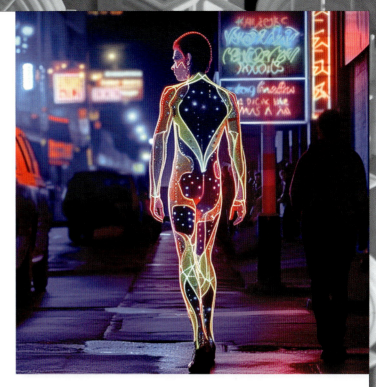

Owen Hopkins,
Bowie in Multispace,
2023

Ziggy Stardust, Aladdin Sane, Halloween Jack, the Thin White Duke – these are just some of the personas David Bowie adopted over his career. As with all the best artists, Bowie revealed what is latent within us, with his multiple personas prefiguring the hybrid identities and existences that define our experience of multispace. This AI-generated image sublimate's Bowie's multiple identities into a single yet fluid figure, constantly in transition, defined by their hybridity.

Multispace exists in the intersection of the physical and digital and in the blurring of their previously clear dividing lines. Multispace is not a single space, but a hybrid space where we are, in effect, occupying multiple spaces simultaneously

Enlightenment of the 17th and 18th centuries. Rational/irrational, truth/untruth, us/them – it is not that these categories do not exist; rather, where there was once a stark divide between them, there is now a vast, undulating overlap. All is contingent, so much so that the very idea of individual intellectual autonomy, of free will itself, on which the total weight of Enlightenment thought was laid, is no longer an absolute. In the world of Google Autocomplete, the algorithm knows us better than we know ourselves.

Architecture, which not coincidentally emerged in its modern form with the Enlightenment, has as a discipline depended more than most on the starkness of these binary distinctions. At its simplest form, to delineate and enclose a volume – to create a space, at least in one sense of the word – is to define what is inside/outside, what is included/excluded, and by implication the human/natural worlds. Thus, the very notion of multispace – where the spaces we occupy fold into themselves and are dynamic, with their extent ever changing – throws architecture itself into question, philosophically and practically.

This is ironic, because multispace was there at architecture's beginning. The seeds of architecture's disciplinary demise were sown at its formation. One of the first consciously fabricated multispaces is the house of the English architect Sir John Soane, on Lincoln's Inn Fields in London. Its present status as a 'museum' is a misnomer. For if a museum of the Enlightenment or otherwise is, traditionally speaking, a stable entity with one single narrative, what Soane created was a space of multiplicity – of many, sometimes competing references, layers and contexts turned in on themselves, blurring the real and the simulacra to such an extent that there is no meaningful distinction between the two. The Soane 'Museum' is the prototypical multispace; a multispace *avant la lettre*.

Keiichi Matsuda,
Still from *Hyper-Reality*,
2016

Filmed on location in Medellín, Colombia, *Hyper-Reality* is a short, 6-minute concept film shot through the eyes of a young woman as she navigates the city. Everything she sees and experiences is overlaid by augmented reality (AR), turning her journey from bus to supermarket to simply walking down the street into a riot of colour and attention-seeking graphics. For Matsuda, the film is an attempt to envision the exciting new kinds of experiences these technologies will offer, while acting as a warning of some of their more troubling implications.

All multispaces are equally defined by the simultaneity of the physical and the digital

ScanLAB,
3D scan of Sir John Soane's Museum,
London,
2016

In 1780, John Soane set off back to England after spending two highly formative years in Italy on the Grand Tour. Tragically for the young Soane, while travelling over the Alps his trunk came open and he lost all the notes and sketches he had scrupulously made while away. Thus, Soane's experience was confined to his memory. Years later, he in effect re-spatialised these memories in his museum's complex, multi-planar and multidimensional composition of objects in space. The museum is incredibly well recorded, yet 3D scanning is arguably the only representational media that captures its multispatial quality.

Forms of Multispace

Such proto-multispaces were exceptional in the pre-digital era. Now, as the digital has become interwoven in almost every aspect of human activity, multispaces are the norm. While only a few years ago we entered multispace only occasionally or in very particular circumstances, today it is pervasive. Varying in both medium and intensity, multispace by definition takes multiple forms, yet all multispaces are equally defined by the simultaneity of the physical and the digital.

Nascent augmented reality (AR), where our experience of the physical world is mediated by digital overlays, offers perhaps the clearest expression of multispace. For the moment, such experiences are confined to phone screens, or to virtual reality (VR) goggles and cameras where we are not looking at the world but a real-time video of it onto/into which are inserted virtual objects or layers. Even with the arrival of the ground-breaking Apple Vision Pro, much work is still to be done for this technology to become as straightforward as wearing a pair of glasses – the technological holy grail – but this is the logical progression.

The technological seamlessness this heralds is already a hallmark of many forms of multispace. We enter multispace when we join a Zoom call, when we are both sat in our office and in a digital space with people from all over the world.

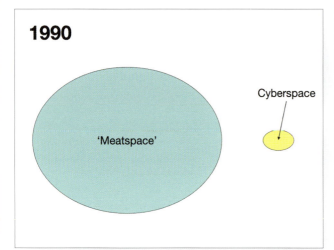
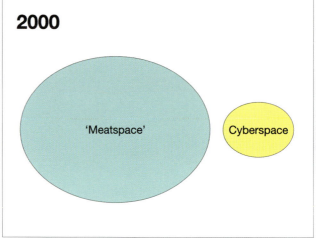
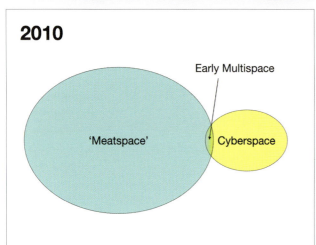
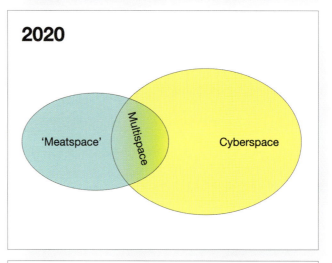
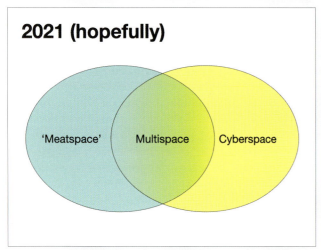
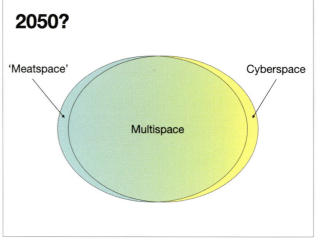

Owen Hopkins,
Multispace diagram,
2021

above: The concept of multispace arose as a BA dissertation elective at Newcastle University in early 2021, partly in response to the pandemic's enforced shift of human interaction – including, most significantly here, university teaching – to the digital platforms. This consciously crude diagram produced at the time illustrates the trajectory of the interaction and overlap of physical and digital realities – here described as 'meatspace' and 'cyberspace' – looking back and also looking forward.

Cover of ⌂ Architects in Cyberspace,
November/December
1995

right: Architecture's readiness to embrace digital technologies in the design and production of buildings contrasts with the way it has largely ignored their effects on how we experience them. This ⌂ issue, on multispace, is just the latest attempt to rectify this. Indeed, Martin Pearce's closing remark in his introduction to Architects in Cyberspace, guest-edited with Neil Spiller, is as relevant now as it was then: 'While the contributors raise both the potentials and the pitfalls that we may encounter, we need to ask if we will be able to find the tools, not least ethical and moral, that will navigate us into the uncertain future and shape it in the way we desire.'

'Kitten Zoom Filter Mishap',
9 February 2021

'I'm here live. I'm not a cat' – the now immortal words of attorney Rod Ponton, spoken at a civil forfeiture hearing at Texas's 394th Judicial District Court. Due to pandemic social distancing, the hearing was taking place via Zoom. Ponton joined the call with a white kitten face filter which he struggled to remove, while the other participants on the call looked on with little reaction despite the hilarity of what was taking place. The clip went 'viral' and appeared on numerous major news outlets.

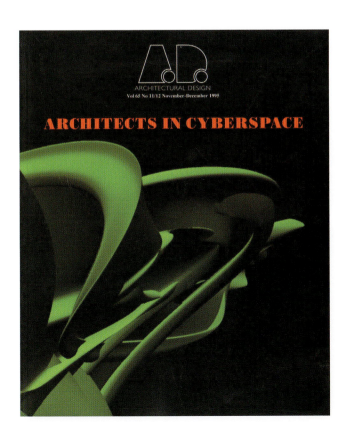

Multispace is simultaneously public and private; we can be sat in our bedrooms playing a PC game while streaming it live to thousands via Twitch. Multispace is both simultaneous, as in the previous two examples, and asynchronous, such as when we are cycling down a country lane while racing against thousands of other people who also use the Strava app.

Multispace redefines how we understand proximity. In multispace we are together and alone at the same time. We can be sat on our sofa watching a television show while taking part in a Twitter conversation with thousands. In other instances, the situation is reversed. In 2016, crowds of people would spontaneously appear in strange locations in cities across the world, seemingly for no reason – that is, unless you knew there had been a sighting at that location of a sought-after Pokémon, which existed only on smartphone screens.

We rarely need to actively enter multispace. We are in multispace when we are driving down a road and the GPS tells us there is traffic ahead after detecting a number of smartphones moving slowly in close proximity. In fact, we are in multispace whenever and wherever we have a smartphone in our pocket passively counting our steps and signalling our location, while wearers of smartwatches are in multispace even when they sleep. With the number of active smartphones in the world beginning to rival total global population, it is no exaggeration to say that in vast swathes of contemporary life there is no longer any meaningful distinction between physical and digital spaces. There is only multispace.

After Architecture

The profound and far-reaching changes in how we experience and understand the world that multispace has brought about herald equally profound and far-reaching changes for architecture as a practice that engages with and attempts to shape it. How do we understand site in multispace when physical proximities are interwoven with digital ones? What about context – the conceptual touchstone for almost all branches of architecture – which becomes both local and dislocated, simultaneously micro and macro in scale?

Then there is a building's surface appearance, which is no longer fixed but can be overlaid in real time and infinitely customised. What do aesthetics and style mean when architecture becomes an individualised rather than shared experience? How does the consequent separation of a building's 'use-value' and 'symbolic-value' alter architecture's approaches to structure, materials and form? And, pivotally, how is multispace's new arena of architectural experience determined by social, economic, racial and geographical imbalances? Does it entrench existing divisions or offer ways out of them?

Architecture has, for the most part, been lamentably slow in retooling itself to be able to address these transformations. And this, in part, is what this issue of △ aims to help rectify. But simply expanding architecture's field of enquiry into the digital, as well as the material, while important and necessary, is not enough. Multispace's impact on architecture runs much deeper, destabilising the philosophical underpinnings that have supported it for at least the last three centuries. New, supplemental approaches, methodologies and sensibilities must be developed to create a hybrid discipline able to address the full scope of the hybrid world in which it operates.

This issue brings together a range of practitioners and thinkers who are involved in doing just that: developing ideas, approaches and positions that coalesce around what might be described as the 'post-architectural'. It begins with three articles by practitioners tackling the architectural dynamics of multispace. Lara Lesmes and Fredrik Hellberg of Space Popular explore the thresholds between the physical and the digital, while Lucia Tahan extrapolates the new spatial languages that emerge in their intersection, and Wendy W Fok considers the architectural codings of the material infrastructures that underpin them.

Though architectural in conception, multispace offers new ways of experiencing the world that cut across much of what we conventionally consider as architectural. Writer and curator Jesse Damiani delves into how artists are articulating the contemporary multivalent, decentralised condition of 'post-reality'. Architectural designer and researcher Paula Strunden discusses the multisensory experiences of multispace through her research constructing extended-reality models. Historian and narrative designer Holly Nielsen takes the long view in her exploration of new forms and practices of domesticity that emerge through multispace.

This thread is picked up by architect and researcher Giacomo Pala in his theoretical reconstitution of space as a series of dynamic and often competing conjunctions. For artist-architect Ibiye Camp, digital technologies, notably photogrammetry, offer ways to foreground more inclusive understandings of spaces often overlooked by conventional/Western architectural approaches. Joshua Bard and Francesca Torello, both educators at the School of Architecture at Carnegie Mellon University in Pennsylvania, look back to move forward, considering how multispace exposes the 'latent virtuality' inherent to greater or lesser extents in all architecture, while architect and educator Andrew Kovacs looks at the multispatial potentials of public art in allowing multiple ideas, narratives and power structures to coexist and interact.

Multispace changes how we see the world as it is, but also opens up the potential for the realisation of new, more equitable hybrid worlds. Writer Alice Bucknell explores how 'world-building' by artists and gamers can act as a tool for visualising multiple near-futures. Sasha Belitskaja, of the iheartblob extended-reality and architecture studio, argues that despite their disciplinary inertia, architects are uniquely well positioned to help us define and navigate multispace. Scholar and activist Micaela Mantegna and AI architecture and strategy consultant Marcelo Rinesi consider the ethical implications of multispaces and the need to resist big tech's inevitable 'land grab' – a mission in which, the visionary filmmaker Liam Young argues, architects must play a decisive role.

Space Popular (Lara Lesmes and Fredrik Hellberg)
and Owen Hopkins,
ROOT DOMAIN: Tracing the Physical Impact
of Digital Museums and Archives,
2020

A classic 'lockdown project', ROOT DOMAIN was a speculative proposal for a new kind of museum emerging from the equivalence between the way conventional museums are constructed to obscure the power imbalances that sustain them, and how digital technology is designed to distance its users from its environmental impacts. The image shows a mixed-reality (MR) experience where visitors are met with a large sphere floating in mid-air, which quickly reveals itself as a visualisation of the world through the new unfolding geography of data.

Though architectural in conception, multispace offers new ways of experiencing the world that cut across much of what we conventionally consider as architectural

Entering the Post-architectural

There are moments throughout history when architects have taken centre stage in the articulation of new worlds, new ways of thinking and new ways of interacting. If the 21st century is going to be defined by the emerging realities of multispace, then this must be one of those moments. Already, vast commercial forces are in the process of creating neat, isolated walled gardens in the guise of the 'metaverse'. These discrete mono-spaces are not only unaccountably controlled from above, but are actively conceived to disconnect their users from the material and environmental injustices that sustain them and, most damningly, risk simply replicating and quite possibly exacerbating the injustices and power imbalances that define the physical world.

Architecture can change this and ensure this becomes the age not of the metaverse but of multispace – open and pluralistic where multiple experiences, identities and cultures are not just sustained, but actively nurtured. However, this will only be possible by embracing and developing post-architectural positions and practices through which multispace can be articulated, modified, appropriated and assimilated for the benefit of all its users as well as its producers. Although post-architecture constitutes a seismic disciplinary shift, it is not the end of architecture as we know it, but rather its transcendence: repurposing the discipline for the multispatial world in which we now live. ⌂

Note
1. David Bowie speaking to Jeremy Paxman on *BBC Newsnight* in 1999: https://www.youtube.com/watch?v=FiK7s_0tGsg.

Text © 2023 John Wiley & Sons Ltd. Images: p 6 © Adam Nathaniel Furman; pp 7 © Owen Hopkins; pp 8–9(t) © Keiichi Matsuda; p 8(b) Image courtesy ScanLab and Sir John Soane's Museum; p 10 © Owen Hopkins. AI-generated image created in Midjourney; p 11(b) Scan courtesy of Stephen Parnell; pp 12–13 © Space Popular

Lara Lesmes and Fredrik Hellberg

THE PORTAL GALLERIES

RESEARCHING PORTALS IN FICTION FROM THE 19TH CENTURY TO THE PRESENT

Space Popular (Lara Lesmes and Fredrik Hellberg),
Portal archetypes, 2022

The desire to travel virtually across time, space and realms has been a recurring theme in the collective imagination — one that many have explored through fictional narratives. As a result, portals are a popular device in mainstream media: we read about them in books, see them on the screen, and even traverse them in games.

The notion of portals to alternative multispaces where normalcy is subverted into magical situations has been a feature of fiction for centuries. Architects and educators Lara Lesmes and Fredrik Hellberg have catalogued some of these fictive realms and mechanisms, and developed their own augmented-reality portal to show the results of their research.

Space Popular (Lara Lesmes and Fredrik Hellberg), 'The Portal Galleries' exhibition, Sir John Soane's Museum, London, 2022

Some go this way, some go that way, but as for me, myself, personally, I prefer the shortcut.
— the Cheshire Cat in the Disney film *Alice in Wonderland*, 1951[1]

A rabbit hole that leads to Wonderland, a time-travelling police box bigger on the inside, a rainbow that beams you to the land of the gods – the stories we tell are full of magical portals of staggering variety. Some are monumental and mysterious, like the Star Gate monolith from *2001: A Space Odyssey* (1968);[2] others are modest and mad, like the small hidden door in *Being John Malkovich* (1999)[3] which leads to the mind of the eponymous actor.

The word 'portal' can be used to describe a transformative experience like a flashback, often triggered by an object that recalls a memory. It is also used to describe websites that serve as a guide or point of entry, such as Wikipedia. This article concerns the portal as a fictional device like a threshold or doorway that can bend the rules of physics and transport us across time, space or other dimensions – portals that are most commonly found in fantasy and science-fiction books, films, television series and games.

A hundred years ago, in a world caught between two world wars, stories of portals were rare and found mainly in scarce science-fiction novels or, looking back, in local mythologies,

Still from the immersive film *The Portal Galleries, Act 2*. Portals are door-like or hole-like thresholds that grant us entrance into another virtual environment of any kind and size. As digital media gain a third dimension and become immersive, the way in which we swap between spaces will have to be designed. Portals are one of the most popular means to switch from one environment to another and they will likely become the go-to reference for virtual travel.

The Portal Galleries project archive and exhibition aims to compile a history of what will be the key architectural element of the coming decades. Between 2020 and 2022 an archive of portals in fiction was compiled with over 900 entries. The analysis of the archive has already led to initial conclusions and remains an open resource for study.

16

folklore, religious texts and oral histories. By 2023, however, nearly 30 per cent of the top 50 highest-grossing films of all time contained portals.[4] As we consume ever more science fiction and fantasy, portal fiction has emerged from obscurity to the mainstream. Today, we do not require introduction to or explanation of the idea of a multiverse and the ways it might be accessed. The magic and mechanics of multiversal travelling through portals have such well-established tropes and lore that they can be baked into stories with the same ease as a magic wand or even a car.

The multiversification of storytelling can be read as a telling sign that we are collectively trying to envision a life in which physical and virtual experiences are inseparable. Perhaps we already live in a multiverse, we just do not see it as such. Every day we experience spaces our bodies cannot reach. We create media for our senses to travel further and faster than our bodies ever could, and stretch our perception across time and space. Media extend our bodies and minds, yet our cognitive capacity to absorb information and experiences is not as malleable or scalable.

Part of the struggle to process the vast quantity of experiences and exchanges we have every single day is that they are all contained within the same black rectangle. The screen from which we access the internet follows from the tradition of the book in the sense that it compresses information. This book, however, does not contain one story but a myriad of them; it does not have a cover but it must be all covers at once; and it is not found on a library shelf but it contains libraries within. Accessing the entirety of the internet from one single screen means that we cannot *place* the ideas or experiences we are scrolling through. The development of immersive technology such as virtual-reality headsets and augmented-reality devices will allow us to separate, diversify and *place* our digital experiences so they can be comprehensive to our very spatial minds.

With the spatialisation of media will come the necessity to *travel* and to make sense of transitions between spaces, hence the portal. Portals provide a transition that can help us cognitively make sense of the massive leaps we take when we travel virtually. At their best they reconcile the audio-visual experiences enabled by immersive technology with our physical bodies. This is vital because, as we step inside media by means of such technology, all previously two-dimensional elements and interactions become spatial, with the portal becoming a three-dimensional hyperlink acting as a threshold that handles the transition between spaces experientially and practically. The go-to precedents for how to design these transitions will be the huge number of portals in popular culture.

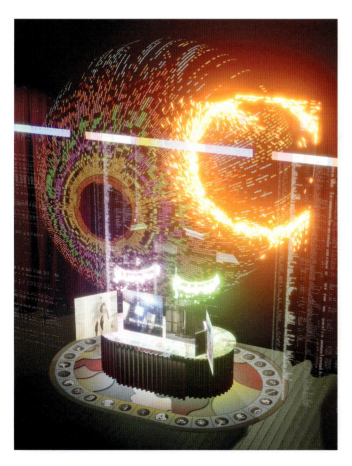

The exhibition and immersive film presented the archive of portals in response to the virtuality of Soane's work, bridging the technologies of his time and ours. Scale shifts, unfolding walls and cleverly placed mirrors are just some of the numerous examples of portals at the museum that is Soane's former home, making it one of the greatest collections of pre-electronic media teleportation devices.

The exhibition consisted of several parts presenting a cross-media historical study of fictional portals: two immersive films with accompanying furniture pieces that enable a multisensory experience, a 2D film presenting the 18 portal archetypes found in the archive, analytical drawings of portals in Sir John Soane's Museum, and a curated series of drawings from Soane's office representing a diversity of thresholds.

Researching Portals

In 2019, Space Popular began building an archive of portals found in fiction through a research project called The Portal Galleries. The findings of the project were first presented at Sir John Soane's Museum in London in 2022 and at MAK, the Museum of Applied Arts in Vienna in 2023, in the form of an immersive film and a timeline. The project brought together over 1,000 portals found in books, films, graphic novels and games in mainly Western popular culture covering the last 250 years. The research covered information about each portal's creation, mechanics, usage and rules, as well as information about the story it belongs to – such as when it first appeared and when it reappeared in sequels or reproductions, the genre it belongs to, its intended audience and the formats in which it was distributed. A series of conclusions were drawn from the observation of patterns in the database, as well as the identification of 18 portal archetypes.

The study draws a difference between portals, teleportation and telepresence. Portals are door-like or hole-like thresholds that we cross with our body to gain entrance into another environment. We consider that a virtual-reality headset provides the experience of telepresence and therefore is not a portal. Neither are the 'plugs' in *The Matrix* (1999),[5] or other simulations that leave the body behind which we also consider examples of telepresence. Teleportation, as popularised in video games and virtual-reality gaming and gathering, is a mechanism through which one can 'jump' through vast distances without the use of a portal. In teleportation there is no transition, which tends to create disorientation for the individual teleporting as well as those around them.

At the start of the study, we expected to encounter portals in stories dating very far back in the form of magic wells, gates to the afterlife and caves leading to parallel worlds. Indeed, portals of the most extravagant kind are found in religious scriptures, mythology and folklore from around the world. Thresholds to the realm of God or gods have, for example, been described through spatial terminology akin to portals in many cases throughout history. However, it was decided that the Portal Galleries project would cover only portals found in fiction and exclude religious scriptures or folklore.

Compared to the incredible number of portals found in popular fiction in the late 20th and early 21st centuries, portals appear infrequently in the 19th century. Where they do appear in the stories from this time, it is often children who cross magical portals with surprising amounts of calm into fantastical lands. In areas with a Christian background, this could be explained by the fact that the Church in its different forms could censor literature which verged towards the magical or 'unnatural'. In the most well-known books of the time, such as Lewis Carroll's *Alice's Adventures in Wonderland* (1865)[6] and L Frank Baum's *The Wonderful Wizard of Oz* (1900),[7] the existence of magical portals and parallel worlds is left ambiguous, as the protagonist – who is often a female child – is the only person who experienced it subjectively in some sort of dream state in which her lucidity could be put into question.

Space Popular (Lara Lesmes and Fredrik Hellberg), Portal studies of Sir John Soane's Museum, 2022

Images exploring the latent virtuality of Sir John Soane's Museum.

Above: a fantasy view of the Picture Room looking back from within one of the many worlds contained in its famous unfolding wall displays.

Opposite left: the passage from the South Drawing Room to the exhibition galleries, a journey from Soane's world back to our own.

Opposite middle and right: explorations of the potential of mirrors located in two of the museum's iconic spaces – the Breakfast Room and Library-Dining Room – to act as portals. (Researcher and illustrator: Rachel Swetnam)

Space Popular (Lara Lesmes and Fredrik Hellberg), 'The Portal Galleries' exhibition, Sir John Soane's Museum, London, 2022

At the centre of the gallery stood a table covered in Alcantara®, which mapped Space Popular's study of portals in fiction and their development throughout time. The piece comprised an immersive film composed on physical and virtual elements, viewed through a virtual-reality headset and matched over a physical table. When experiencing the film, viewers could touch the physical table which was also present – visually – in the immersive film. Here the diagram is dynamic and interactive to the story.

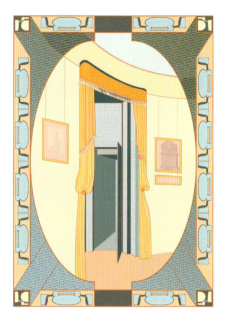
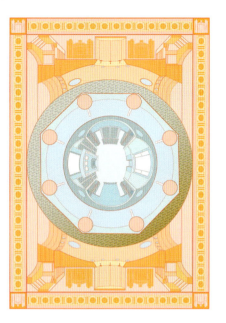
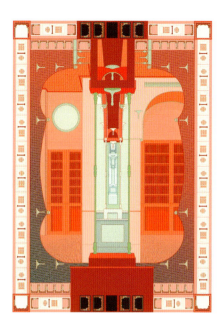

Entering the Portal Era

The period of mass industrialisation, globalisation, secularisation and mass-media explosion that followed the Second World War was when the portal era really began, heralded by Arthur C Clarke's short story *The Sentinel* (1951),[8] which later became the basis for the 1968 film *2001: A Space Odyssey*. The 'WABAC machine' from the 'Peabody's Improbable History' segments of the late 1950s and early 1960s animated series *The Adventures of Rocky and Bullwinkle and Friends*[9] and the 'Tollbooth' from the 1961 book *The Phantom Tollbooth* by architect Norton Juster[10] are other notable examples of that time.

During that time and up until the height of the Cold War and the epoch-defining moment of the Moon landing, portals were often resource-heavy machines powered by science, not magic, and a result of tremendous collaborative efforts, to be used in a race for dominance. Examples include the massive time machine in the 1960s TV series *The Time Tunnel*[11] where thousands of people work under the desert surface on a secret megastructure, codenamed 'Operation Tic-Toc', which would allow the US military to travel in time. Its iconic spiral design has been replicated and mocked through countless subsequent fictional portals such as the time machine in the 1999 film *Austin Powers: The Spy Who Shagged Me*.[12]

In the same period, audiences were also introduced to the 20-kilometre (12-mile) long *Heighliner* starship in the *Dune* books (1965–), films and television series[13] which in the story are used by the Empire and the Spacing Guild to transport people and equipment across the known universe. The fuel that powers this intergalactic portal infrastructure is 'the spice', the most expensive substance in the universe, which is central to the Empire's dominance and control of its vast cosmic domain.

Postmodern to Present-Day Portals

Portals in the form of gigantic machines used as weapons for imperialism that marked the Cold War era gave way during the 1980s to a period where portals were simple but cleverly designed and often served satirical and comical roles in low-brow science fiction, family movies and body horror. The time-travelling DeLorean in *Back to the Future* (1985),[14] the phone booth in *Bill & Ted's Excellent Adventure* (1989)[15] and the people-eating television in *Videodrome* (1983)[16] are all familiar examples of what we might call a Postmodern portal period, full of gags and gore.

The period that followed and largely lasts until today has focused on class, status and ethnic divides. There have been countless stories during this period where portals are out of reach to most and accessible only to a select few. The portals in these stories are often made possible by magic and play an essential part in a power struggle where right of access is granted to a privileged minority, or in more extreme cases only to one race, family or even one single person.

Probably the best-known example is the brick-wall portal leading to platform 9¾ in the *Harry Potter* series,[17] where those who are born into a certain group of people can easily run through the wall into a future of power and privilege while the rest would – symbolically and literally – smash their face against the brick and never know the life on the other side. As in this instance, portals in today's most popular stories are predominantly used as tools to get the upper hand (access, speed, knowledge, weapons, etc) and therefore gain control over others.

At the same time as exclusivity in access to portals escalates, for the privileged few who do have access to them they become ever more casual and integrated into the everyday life of the

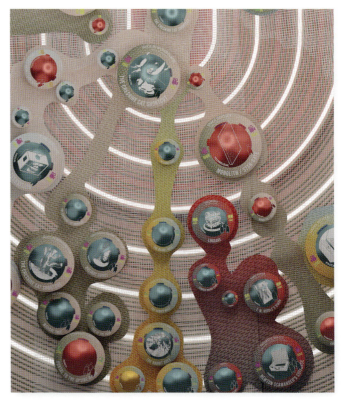

story. The comic-book and latterly film character Doctor Strange[18] uses portals created with the help of a magical ring to unceremoniously reach for a book, while Rick in the animated television series *Rick and Morty* (2013–)[19] uses his technologically advanced portal gun for the most banal and mundane purposes, such as speeding up the ageing process of wine to impress a house guest.

Portals as Virtual Infrastructure

Aside from their presence in fiction, portals are already commonplace elements in video games and social virtual-reality platforms, albeit mostly existing within private platforms and not currently providing a connection between them. And with growing erosion of the distinction between physical and digital lives, we are already foreseeing the tremendous political, technological and cognitive challenges that a life full of portals will bring.

If the 1950s and 1960s were the age of physical infrastructure when portal fiction featured imperial technological warfare and the 1990s and 2010s the age of digital infrastructure when privilege and exclusion drove the desire for magical portals, the 2020s and 2030s will be the time of virtual infrastructure when we actually build portals to be used every day within spatial media.

Portals will be our vessels to sail across virtual environments. Therefore, the way in which these portals operate, the places they connect and how they do it will define the fairness of virtual infrastructure. Studying the portal archetypes found in fiction, their history and their cultural associations is a vital and continuing reference point for the design, regulation and development of portals as they become part of everyday life. △

Notes

1. Clyde Geronimi, Wilfred Jackson and Hamilton Luske (directors), *Alice in Wonderland*, Walt Disney Productions, 1951.
2. Stanley Kubrick (director/co-writer), *2001: A Space Odyssey*, Stanley Kubrick Productions, 1968.
3. Spike Jonze (director), *Being John Malkovich*, Universal Pictures International, 1999.
4. https://en.wikipedia.org/wiki/List_of_highest-grossing_films.
5. The Wachowskis (directors/writers), *The Matrix*, Warner Bros, 1999.
6. Lewis Carroll, *Alice's Adventures in Wonderland*, Macmillan (London), 1865.
7. L Frank Baum, *The Wonderful Wizard of Oz*, George M Hill Co (Chicago and New York), 1900.
8. Arthur C Clarke, 'The Sentinel', first published in *10 Story Fantasy*, Spring 1951.
9. Jay Ward, Alex Anderson and Bill Scott (creators), *The Adventures of Rocky and Bullwinkle and Friends*, originally aired on the ABC and NBC television networks, 1959–64.
10. Norton Juster, *The Phantom Tollbooth*, Epstein & Carroll (New York), 1961.
11. Irwin Allen (creator/producer), *The Time Tunnel*, originally aired on the ABC television network, 1966–7.
12. Jay Roach (director), *Austin Powers: The Spy Who Shagged Me*, Eric's Boy / Team Todd, 1999.
13. Frank Herbert, *Dune*, Chilton Book Co (Boston, MA), 1965, and multiple sequels by Herbert himself, his son Brian Herbert and Kevin J Anderson. The series has sparked various film and television adaptations, most recently in big-screen versions directed and co-written by Denis Villeneuve (2021 and 2023).
14. Robert Zemeckis (director/co-writer), *Back to the Future*, Universal Pictures, 1985.
15. Stephen Herek (director), *Bill & Ted's Excellent Adventure*, Orion Pictures, 1989.
16. David Cronenberg (director/writer), *Videodrome*, Universal Pictures, 1983.
17. JK Rowling, *Harry Potter and the Philosopher's Stone*, Bloomsbury (London), 1997, and its various sequels.
18. Doctor Strange first appeared in Marvel Comics' *Strange Tales* no 110, July 1963.
19. Justin Rolland and Dan Harmon (creators), *Rick and Morty*, Warner Bros Television, 2013–.

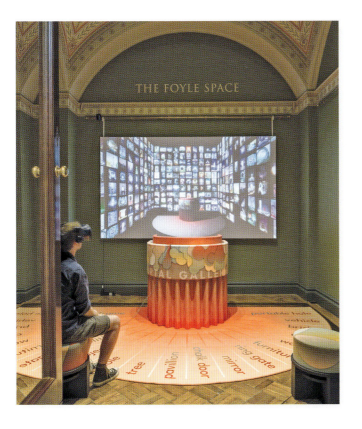

Space Popular (Lara Lesmes and Fredrik Hellberg), 'The Portal Galleries' exhibition, Sir John Soane's Museum, London, 2022

opposite left: Visitors were able to explore surface details highlighting significant examples of portals in media such as books, films and video games, indicating when they appeared and their defining features. The portals were arranged according to a series of archetypes identified in the research.

opposite right: Close inspection of the table revealed how each centimetre represents one year, starting from the 1950s, which saw an explosion of interest in the idea of the portal and the transit it enables, and moving towards the 2020s.

left: Installation shot and still from the immersive film *The Portal Galleries, Act 1*. The first exhibition space visitors encountered having entered the museum was the Foyle Space, located to the side of the iconic Dome area, which is itself a portal-like journey through time and space.

Text © 2023 John Wiley & Sons Ltd. Images: pp 14–18, 19(t), 20(r) © Space Popular; pp 19(b), 21 © Gareth Gardner; p 20(l) Photo by Matthew Blunderfeld

Lucia Tahan

THE HOME AS AN INFINITE SCREEN

Lucia Tahan,
Cloud Housing,
Housing the Human Festival,
Radialsystem,
Berlin,
2019

In the augmented home, augmented-reality (AR) artefacts are displayed over the physical space, including downloaded objects, shortcuts to files, decorative objects and elements that change the room's height and open it to a virtual sky.

The continuing digital tsunami is offering enhanced spatial opportunities for architects. The interaction of real space and virtual space can be choreographed along a spectrum that ranges from our mobile-phone screens to full bodily immersion in digital reality. Architect **Lucia Tahan** exploits these possibilities in her design work using various methods of spatial computing. Here she takes us through some of her recent experiments and thoughts.

Responding to an installation called *Cloud Housing* that I created at Radialsystem, Berlin in 2019, a visitor remarked that when turning off the augmented-reality (AR) layers, the room, which was now devoid of brightly coloured digital objects, enhancements, icons and avatars, looked duller – duller in fact than it had before he had picked up the tablet through which the AR elements could be seen. The visitor had been interacting with my 'reality slider', which gradually alters the number of objects, interfaces and notifications appearing over a physical living-room scene. The slider had been conceived as a metaphor for the gradual transition between physical and digital realities, and also a very realistic representation of the way we will interact with immersive media in the future.

A Spectrum of Realities

The smooth transition between complete immersion (virtual reality) and functional overlay (augmented reality) is a fundamental element of our interaction in immersive technologies. The spatial perception of a screen – a rectangle that exists as an object in our field of view – is replaced by a 'spectrum of realities'. This spectrum corresponds to the ability of the user to switch and transition between levels of digital and physical reality, from seeing only a few digital elements to replacing the physical environment completely.

Lucia Tahan,
Cloud Housing,
Housing the Human Festival,
Radialsystem,
Berlin,
2019

opposite: A reality slider allows users to transition between physical and personal realities that correspond to levels of density and customisation of the digital layers overlaid on the space. Physical reality becomes a pole on a spectrum of immersive media.

below: In this screenshot of the AR application in *Cloud Housing*, two-dimensional interfaces are shown over the physical world. These include notifications and recommendations based on the user's tracked behaviour in their space, such as the hours spent on the sofa.

A convincing spectrum of realities relies on cameras and sensors on devices to understand scenes and bodies. The amount of data that can be collected by these devices is enormous and poses profound privacy-related questions. Which spatial data is more or less private: pixels, meshes, people? How can it be misused? It seems likely that because of these privacy concerns and the social (un)acceptability of wearing head-mounted displays (HMDs) or headsets in public, immersive technologies will likely be primarily a domestic instrument throwing into question current understandings of domesticity.

Yet even now, a straightforward mapping of a private–public dichotomy on to domestic–non-domestic spaces seems naive. After all, the very notion of home interiors as a strictly private space is relatively new, dating only from the 19th century. And it may well be that immersive technologies are actually posing a return to pre-modern understandings of domesticity.

Either way, immersive technologies bring public space and, by implication the spatial quality of the city, into the home, allowing for the creation of, and access to myriad hybrid spaces or realities, all of which poses numerous urgent and far-reaching questions. How might the emergence of premium realities, advertisement realities, free realities, sample realities exacerbate inequalities by fragmenting access to spatial

quality? Should users subscribe to realities, creators of realities or reality platforms? Who can effectively manage and distribute these realities? NFTs (digital ownership certificates) allow users to own digital objects, thereby moving their possessions from one platform to another, but what rules must objects created by different actors follow so that they can coexist in space in a coherent manner? The answers to many of these questions touches so profoundly on matters of spatial design, philosophy, sociology and politics that it is clear that a technology-only approach is insufficient.

Spatial Computing is an Architectural Discipline
From the point of view of technology, immersive systems constitute an infinite screen. But from that of architecture, immersive technologies offer instant architectural design. They theoretically allow a space to be changed to any design possible as many times as desired. It could be changing the view from a window, making partitions transparent, turning a basement ceiling into that of a cathedral or, beyond the qualities of the space itself, rendering people near each other even when they are far from each other.

Spatial computing is fundamentally an architectural discipline. When viewed through an immersive lens, the home transcends its own physical reality to become the canvas of another reality. Its form limits and affects digital overlays to such an extent that the home itself becomes the screen. The question that immediately arises is, how is a home designed when it is conceived as a screen? And, perhaps more fundamentally, what drives the desire to do this, to install one reality on to another?

Homes as Stages for Media
Historically, the notion that architectural form can be an expression of content and information goes back to the Middle Ages. In their accompanying publication to the 'Database, Network, Interface: The Architecture of Information' exhibition held at Archizoom, Lausanne, in 2021, the curators Mariabruna Fabrizi and Fosco Lucarelli argued that 'throughout human history, the library, the archive and the museum have embodied knowledge, information and collective culture to such an extent that it is possible to compare systems of information organisation with spatial and architectural typologies'.[1]

But the proposition of the home as a screen goes beyond this and associates it with modern content-vessel typologies: the white cube and the black box. The white cube represents the gallery, where architecture recedes into a regular, white-walled, evenly illuminated canvas to contain art. The black box represents the cinema, the game arcade, where architecture is made to disappear via darkness. Will the home become more like either of these models? It seems unlikely. The advancement of immersive technologies is not a radical process – it does not erase what already exists. For the most part, they reference existing screen-based technologies and do not remove the desire for material spatial quality and the emotional and social functions of a home. But at the same time, they generate new possibilities for an architecture of the ephemeral, the ultra-personal, of the collapse of spatial and temporal distance.

Digital media also enables the home to become a more public space than it was before. Video-calling and social media have opened up domestic interiors to the eyes of digital visitors on a daily basis, which in turn has promoted a desire to design and curate domestic spaces to be seen through those lenses. From viral furniture to pristine video-calling backgrounds, home interiors have become a form of social signalling and expression in public contexts.

Lucia Tahan, Irene Iglesias and
Andrea Lusquiños,
Pool House,
Extremadura, Spain,
2018

Domestic and non-domestic spaces do not necessarily map to public and private spaces. The client of this house required an indoor pool in the main living area as a public space that would attract neighbours to bathe and talk. What new forms of public space will arise in domestic spaces when immersive technologies are pervasive?

From viral furniture to pristine video-calling backgrounds, home interiors have become a form of social signalling and expression in public contexts

New Spatial Languages

The architectural discipline has long been aware that architectural languages impart meaning. Over the past few years, a new language has emerged from the medium of the mobile internet. Different platforms have created new formats, such as the post, the tweet or the viral video. These formats, which have enabled the rise of the concept of content and the profession of content creator, enable expression in structured, sortable ways raising significant questions for architecture. What are the current formats for spatial expression in our world, beyond formal architecture? What will be the future, digitally mediated formats for spatial content in an immersive system?

    These were some of the questions I asked in a piece called *Internet Syntax*, part of the 'Ecologies for Other Architectures' exhibition held at La Casa Encendida, Madrid, in 2022, and later at 'Somia La Ciutat' held at the Palau Robert, Barcelona, in 2023, which examined communication content formats such as the emoji, the post, the game, the meme and the reaction. If homes will double as a canvas for immersive content, how will they influence and in turn be influenced themselves by new spatial content types? What formats will be available for spatial content – objects, environments, spatial memories? What forms of spatial expression and design that were not possible until now will be possible in the future?

Lucia Tahan,
Internet Syntax,
'Ecologies for Other Architectures' exhibition, La Casa Encendida, Madrid,
2022

Consisting of a physical object and an AR layer, this piece examined present elements of the language of the internet to ask questions about a future, spatial digital language. The physical cylinder represents the pillar of internet media – its language – while the orbiting satellite cloud of syntactical elements represents its spatialisation.

Lucia Tahan,
Cinema Nervi,
'Pier Luigi Nervi and Florence,
the Structure of Beauty' exhibition,
Manifattura Tabacchi,
Florence,
2021

Immersive technology is an artefact that shows what is distant by hiding what is close. In a homage to Pier Luigi Nervi's work, an element of his structure for the Palazzo del Lavoro was offered as an AR object to be placed in public spaces, commenting on the power of immersive media to collapse spatial and temporal distance.

In architecture, the tectonic and geometrical qualities of an object are intimately joined. But in immersive technology, physics are optional. They are a simulation, decoupled from the object's geometry. There is no real gravity, materials, light or shadows. Designing AR is like taking a knife at the intersection of physics and geometry. Designing the foundations of spatial computing revolves around deciding where to reference the physical world, where to reference screen-based media, and where to break free from both.

The imbrication of physical and digital realities that started with the rise of digital media will accelerate and become more complex with the emergence of immersive technology. Because of the spatial nature of immersive media, architects are in a critical position to pioneer and aid in the design of its foundations and rules. The discipline's values, historical notions and critical potential make architects uniquely equipped to set immersive technology on a fairer and more thoughtful course, while it presents them with an exciting opportunity to expand the limits of architectural design. 𝒟

Note
1. Mariabruna Fabrizi and Fosco Lucarelli, *Database, Network, Interface: The Architecture of Information*, Caryatide (Lausanne), 2021, p 2.

Text © 2023 John Wiley & Sons Ltd. Images: pp 22–7, 29 © Lucia Tahan; p 28 Photo Asier Rua

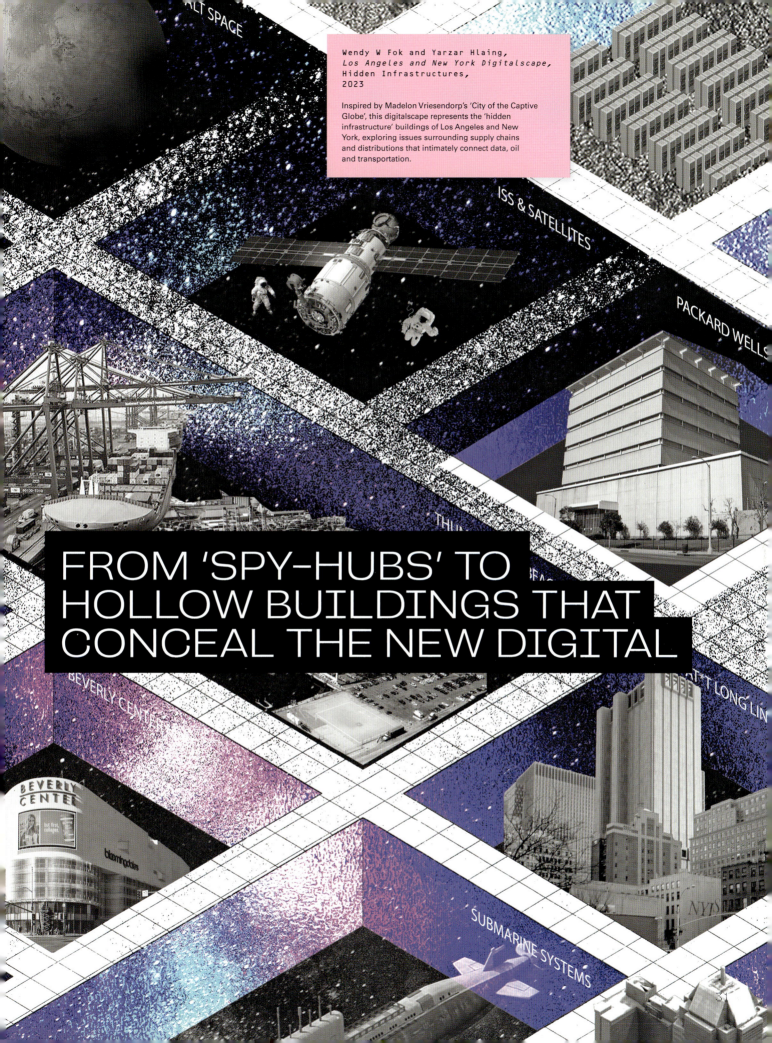

Wendy W Fok and Yarzar Hlaing,
Los Angeles and New York Digitalscape,
Hidden Infrastructures,
2023

Inspired by Madelon Vriesendorp's 'City of the Captive Globe', this digitalscape represents the 'hidden infrastructure' buildings of Los Angeles and New York, exploring issues surrounding supply chains and distributions that intimately connect data, oil and transportation.

FROM 'SPY-HUBS' TO HOLLOW BUILDINGS THAT CONCEAL THE NEW DIGITAL

There are many examples of large technological infrastructure insinuating its unsightly or bland but big manifestations in our cities, and clandestinely covering itself in deceitful architectural details and typologies. Architect and academic **Wendy W Fok** co-led the collaborative Hidden Infrastuctures project, which reveals these tactics, used by both data and extraction technologies, to illustrate a world of subterfuge where all is not what it seems.

Wendy W Fok and Jessica Marquez,
Divided IRT Vent Building,
58 Joralemon Street,
Brooklyn, NY,
Hidden Infrastructures,
2023

opposite top: Coming off as a historical townhouse, 58 Joralemon Street is a secret subway exit and shaft house owned by the Metropolitan Transport Authority (MTA). Originally constructed in 1847, the Greek Revival structure known as the Joralemon Street Tunnel was an extension of the Interborough Rapid Transit Company's (IRT's) first subway line from the Bowling Green station in Manhattan to the IRT Eastern Parkway Line in Brooklyn.

Wendy W Fok and Lucy C Liu,
Spliced Packard Well Site,
Los Angeles, CA,
Hidden Infrastructures,
2023

opposite bottom: The Packard Well Site is an active oil-drilling site disguised at street level as a nondescript office and residential building. Designed like an aircraft hangar, the building is a hollow shell: the interior is a space open to the sky where a derrick is free to move about on tracks, accessing any of the 50 wells in operation.

If you have a smartphone in your pocket or a smartwatch on your wrist, then every movement you make, every interaction you have, creates data. As a result, on a global scale, the amount of data created daily is growing exponentially. All of this data requires physical storage. Some can be stored locally on a smartphone, laptop or any other device that has memory, but there is a limit to the number of files and information that each device can hold. Most ends up in the 'cloud' – a term conceived to simplify the technological realities to which it is connected, but which is actually a systemic infrastructure of cables, conduits and data centres spanning the globe.

If data is the new oil – the fuel that is going to drive the next phase of global economic expansion – then the submarine internet cables that crawl the depths of the ocean and connect societies across continents and oceans, commonly known as the digital infra- or substructure, are the equivalent to oil rigs and their own undersea infrastructure. And like oil rigs, these underwater data cables take a dramatic toll on marine life, as their installation requires dredging and damaging the seabed.[1]

This infrastructure – digital and fossil fuel – and its deleterious effects on the environment are easy to hide when they are at the bottom of the ocean, but much harder when the infrastructure is part of our cities, part of our urban experience. Yet this is precisely what both oil and tech industries have long sought to do, frequently via architectural means.

Hidden Infrastructures is a novel exploration of this phenomenon, documenting the tactics of architectural disguise in infrastructural buildings serving the data (tech) and fossil fuel (oil) industries in the cities and suburbs of Los Angeles and New York. In both cities, these buildings may bear a formal resemblance to a familiar architectural typology on the outside but are created with an entirely different intention on the inside. Many are designed to be utilitarian and functional, but some are conceived to conceal their actual use.

Examples of the phenomenon go back decades. In New York City, home of the oldest underground railway system in the US, the Metropolitan Transit Authority (MTA) – which dates to the mid-1960s – uses a scatter of decommissioned brownstones in pristine, serene and tranquil areas of Manhattan, Brooklyn, Queens and the Bronx as subway air vents to mask infrastructural blight.

Meanwhile, on the West Coast, Los Angeles is home to a plethora of hidden oil wells, such as the Packard Well Site which is camouflaged as an office within the historical Wilshire Vista neighbourhood. Looking sideways for a moment, it does not seem a coincidence that California is also the birthplace of the Advanced Research Projects Agency Network (ARPANET), whose history directly impacts the computational interconnectivity of our modern supply chain. The birth(place) of the internet and data economy is directly intertwined with the fossil-fuel-driven economic trajectory of California as a state.

Architects, alongside property developers and city planners, have at least since the 1960s played a decisive role in creating this phenomenon, deploying uncannily 'common' architectural styles and typologies to disguise infrastructural buildings in urban and suburban communities. The focus of the ongoing research has been on unveiling these resultant hidden infrastructures: identifying, documenting and diagrammatically drawing them out at a range of scales.

Data-Driven Planetary Governance
This work is all the more vital given how these tactics are increasingly being used and extended by tech companies to conceal burgeoning digital infrastructures. For example, veiled as an everyday commercial real-estate office building in the heart of Downtown Los Angeles's Financial District is One Wilshire, which was built originally as an office building and now houses the vital premier communications hub of the Pacific Rim. Not that we would know it from the outside.[2]

Why does this matter? Well, we already have evidence of what happens when telecommunications infrastructure hides in plain sight, with examples of various buildings operating cloaked in mystery, concealing their actual function. One of the most notable examples is the windowless AT&T Long Lines Building (also known as Project X), situated on 33 Thomas Street in New York City. Commissioned during the Cold War and completed in 1974, it was designed by John Carl Warnecke as a 'skyscraper to be inhabited by machines'.[3]

National Security Agency (NSA) documents from 2012–13 indicate that the structure may have also been part of the organisation's surveillance programme (BLARNEY). As reported by *The Intercept*, these documents suggest that the telecommunications operations conducted at 33 Thomas Street were central to a spy hub named TITANPOINTE, which leveraged 'commercial partnerships' to 'gain access and exploit foreign intelligence obtained from global networks'. Architectural floor plans reveal that the building has three subterranean levels, which include a cable vault, that likely led to cable networks beneath Manhattan's streets.[4]

Historically it has been governments who are hungry for our data, but today they have been supplanted by private companies, notably the US tech giants: Alphabet (Google), Microsoft, Meta (Facebook), Amazon and Apple. While these five mega-corporations currently rule the roost, they are being rapidly joined by Chinese companies where the government/private-sector distinction is rather more blurred.

But at least for now, as Sarah Williams, Associate Director of Technology and Urban Planning at the Massachusetts Institute of Technology (MIT), highlights in her book *Data Action* (2020), 'data and many of the insights it offers are gathered by private institutions, responsibilities once attributed to the state are now taken on by private agencies'.[5] And all the tech giants are increasingly investing in data collection and the physical infrastructures it requires, from submarine internet cables to data centres, in some instances going as far as to build their own power stations to run them.

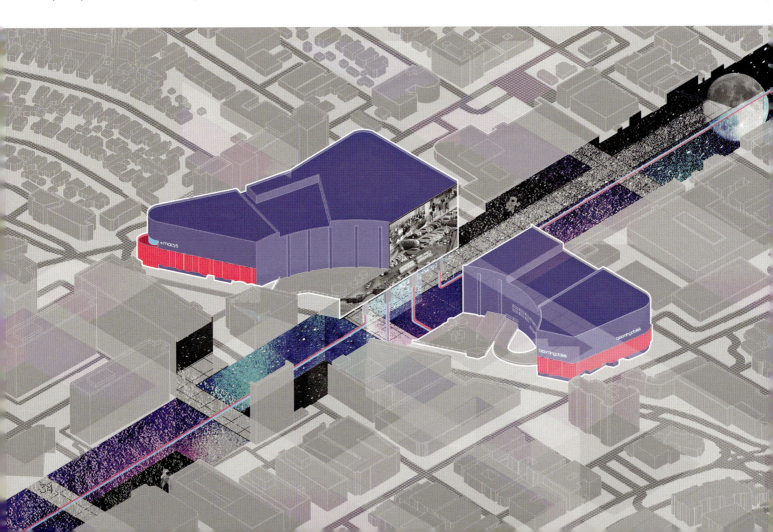

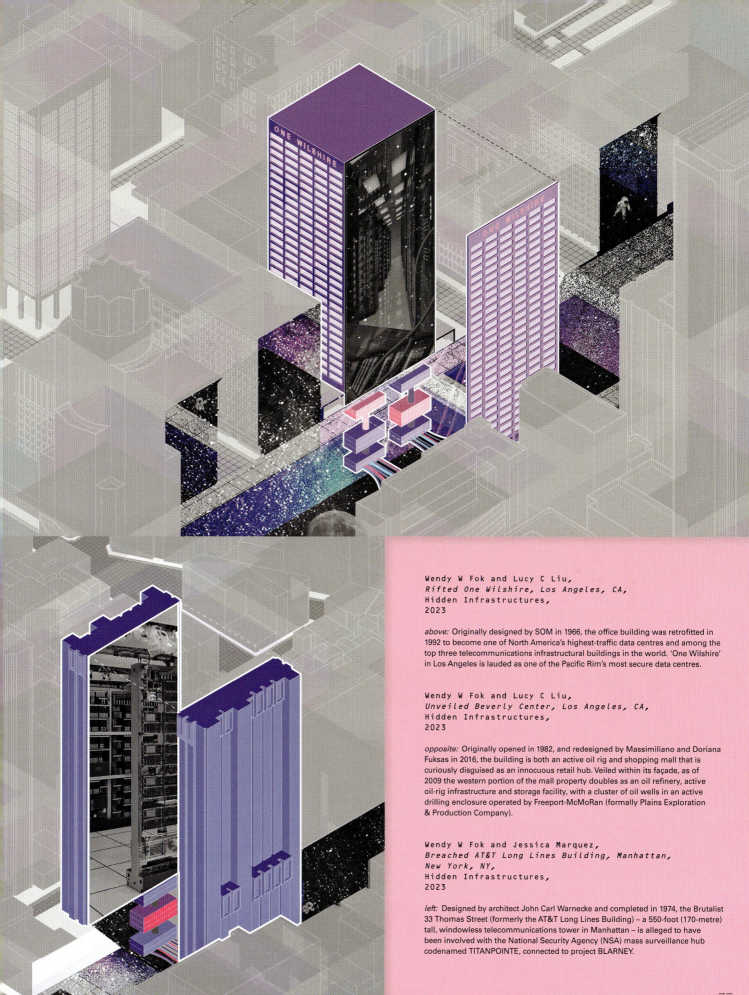

Wendy W Fok and Lucy C Liu,
Rifted One Wilshire, Los Angeles, CA,
Hidden Infrastructures,
2023

above: Originally designed by SOM in 1966, the office building was retrofitted in 1992 to become one of North America's highest-traffic data centres and among the top three telecommunications infrastructural buildings in the world. 'One Wilshire' in Los Angeles is lauded as one of the Pacific Rim's most secure data centres.

Wendy W Fok and Lucy C Liu,
Unveiled Beverly Center, Los Angeles, CA,
Hidden Infrastructures,
2023

opposite: Originally opened in 1982, and redesigned by Massimiliano and Doriana Fuksas in 2016, the building is both an active oil rig and shopping mall that is curiously disguised as an innocuous retail hub. Veiled within its façade, as of 2009 the western portion of the mall property doubles as an oil refinery, active oil-rig infrastructure and storage facility, with a cluster of oil wells in an active drilling enclosure operated by Freeport-McMoRan (formally Plains Exploration & Production Company).

Wendy W Fok and Jessica Marquez,
Breached AT&T Long Lines Building, Manhattan,
New York, NY,
Hidden Infrastructures,
2023

left: Designed by architect John Carl Warnecke and completed in 1974, the Brutalist 33 Thomas Street (formerly the AT&T Long Lines Building) – a 550-foot (170-metre) tall, windowless telecommunications tower in Manhattan – is alleged to have been involved with the National Security Agency (NSA) mass surveillance hub codenamed TITANPOINTE, connected to project BLARNEY.

Wendy W Fok and Jessica Marquez,
*Fissured Intergate Manhattan by Sabey,
New York, NY,
Hidden Infrastructures,*
2023

Number 375 Pearl Street was originally built as a 32-storey office building, commissioned by the New York Telephone Company and completed in 1975. Since then, the building has gone through several iterations of use and ownership, with renovations that started in 2016 transforming it into a mixed-use data centre and office development.

Wendy W Fok, Yvonne Fu and Lin Zhu,
Live with Data,
2021/2022

A novel interpretation of bringing people and data closer together in a physical sense, these pieces are designed as an innovative source of energy enabling people to create value from the otherwise wasted heat of localised micro data centres in their own homes, while allowing them to be at arm's length with their data.

Digital Urbanity in Disguise

This is one thing when data centres are located in remote areas (where land and energy is cheap) but quite another when they are in cities. From an anthropological perspective, urban digital infrastructures raise myriad questions about community, demographics and equity. Who should be living amongst the machine hum of data centres? How would people's sense of neighbourhood change when their houses stand side by side with what are in effect posthuman architectures? Given this, it is no surprise that urban data centres strive for invisibility.

Every time a city government allows a tech company to build warehouses (either for storing physical goods or digital data), that city is choosing 'machine' over 'man', and money over environment. To take just one example, reports in 2021 warned that data centres might cause water shortages for the residents of northern Holland. Although the claim was disputed by the local government, it has raised concerns about the impact of water consumption by ever-growing data centres in our rapidly warming world.

As architects aid the construction of growing numbers of data centres and digital infrastructural buildings that bear an uncanny resemblance to 'everyday' architecture, they are choosing a specific yet highly speculative method of designing the urban landscape of the future.[6] What would the effect be on urban cultures if our neighbours were not human, but rather white picket-fenced houses made to look like any other household, yet populated solely by machines and data?

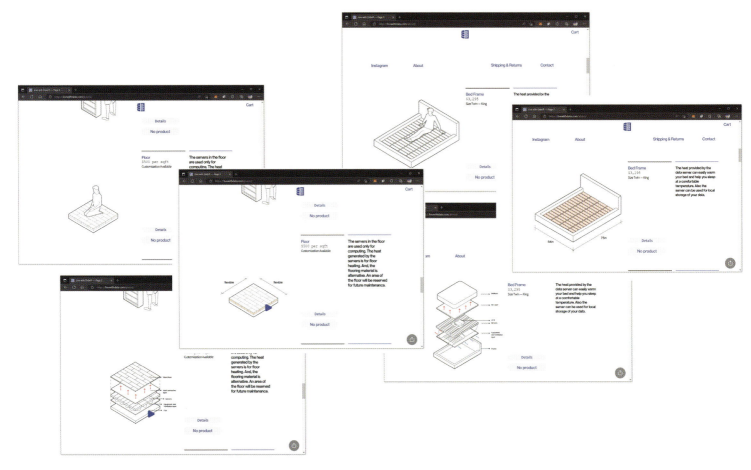

Digital Domesticity
So what are the alternatives? The premise of hidden infrastructures to conceal and integrate infrastructural buildings into residential neighbourhoods may well be a better solution than exporting data centres to foreign and most likely developing countries. Offshoring digital infrastructures raises the same ethical and environmental implications as offshoring carbon emissions. Furthermore, urban locations are also preferable to constructing new data centres in the natural environment. Building hydro-submerged data storage in the ocean, for example, has significant effects on marine life,[7] while running geothermal-powered centres in volcanic regions of El Salvador in order to appease expatriate cryptocurrency development is simply exploitative.

One opportunity can be found in how emerging technologies are paving the way for new domestic relationships and experiences. The conditions under which American suburbia was born have changed dramatically, yet remnants of the 1950s view of domesticity and community linger. Urban planning has become smarter, and has placed ever greater emphasis on community, integration, ecological concerns and quality of life. Yet what may get lost in intelligent urban planning initiatives is the condition of the home, and the feedback loop between the domestic scale of the house and its neighbourhood.

This led to Live with Data, a novel physical and 'real-life' industrial design and interior architecture research project that originated from several years of design development that engages with furniture at a scale of a 'data + user partnership' to playfully question the ways data infrastructure is hidden – or made manifest. The project proposes a system that allows citizens to live with their data in both a decentralised and centralised manner. For example, servers could be integrated into tables, cupboards, sofas, even beds, with the heat generated used to keep the living space warm and dry. Alternatively, or in addition they could be integrated into the building itself via structural insulated panels (SIPs) within the walls or floors of homes.

The premise is simple: what if people were to engage with the data centres in their pure state, as objects within their interiors and integrated into their daily structural framework? The result would be to make our data present and connect our digital experiences with their material implications.

Infrastructural Multispace
Digital domesticity can help but it is at best only a partial solution. The reliance on tech to power businesses and people's day-to-day lives will inevitably increase data processing and storage needs, with the result that more and more of our cities will be given over to digital infrastructure. Will the role of architects in shaping this be reduced to simply finding novel ways to hide or disguise this growing infrastructure, or is there space to put forward more imaginative, progressive and inclusive ways of not just accommodating it but integrating it into our daily lives?

Although data consumption and sustainability would appear to be at opposite ends of the spectrum, momentum is shifting towards greener, more sustainable forms of cloud computing. As more consumers demand that companies play a proactive role in reducing their emissions, they compel big-tech companies and cloud providers to address this.[8] From this emerge numerous possibilities that once again issue from the relationship between digital and fossil-fuel infrastructures.

With the transition from fossil-fuel-powered to electric vehicles, electric charging stations will become ever more part of our cityscapes. What might this change mean for the structure and function of the soon-to-be-obsolete petrol stations (and supporting infrastructures) across the US and beyond? The reusing of sites that facilitated the storage and delivery of the fuel that drove one industrial revolution for the one that is driving the next has logic and also a certain poetry. Rather than hide digital infrastructures, they are brought into the foreground as the physical manifestation of our increasingly multispatial urban existences.

Although many US cities were founded on oil money and driven by oil, they are rapidly shifting to data. To invent new architectural typologies to reflect this, architects need to investigate the hidden typologies of the past. It is the responsibility of designers and architects to design more community-engaged buildings and experiences that better embed the uncanny connective tissues of physical and digital data centres into everyday life. The march towards 'hidden infrastructures' must be halted in order to bring about a more resilient future where data is not distanced from the communities that generate and own it, but is integrated with them. ᴆ

Notes
1. Doug Brake, *Submarine Cables: Critical Infrastructure for Global Communications*, Information Technology and Innovation Foundation (ITIF) Policy Report, April 2019.
2. Kazys Varnelis, 'Eyes That Do Not See: Tracking the Self in the Age of the Data Center', *Harvard Design Magazine*, no 38: *Do You Read Me?*, 2014: https://www.harvarddesignmagazine.com/issues/38/eyes-that-do-not-see-tracking-the-self-in-the-age-of-the-data-center.
3. Jim Dwyer, 'National Security Agency Said to Use Manhattan Tower as Listening Post', *The New York Times*, 18 November 2016: https://www.nytimes.com/2016/11/18/nyregion/national-security-agency-said-to-use-manhattan-tower-as-listening-post.html.
4. Ryan Gallagher and Henrik Moltke, 'Titanpointe: The NSA's Spy Hub in New York, Hidden in Plain Sight', *The Intercept*, 16 November 2016: https://theintercept.com/2016/11/16/the-nsas-spy-hub-in-new-york-hidden-in-plain-sight/.
5. Sarah Williams, 'Data Colonialism', in *Data Action: Using Data for Public Good*, MIT Press (Cambridge, MA), 2020, p 192.
6. Wendy W Fok, 'Megastructures and Infrastructures: The Internet as Megastructure', in *digitalSTRUCTURES: Data and Urban Strategies of the Civic Future*, ORO Editions (Novato, CA), 2023, pp 54–93.
7. See Christina Dunbar-Hester, *Oil Beach: How Toxic Infrastructure Threatens Life in the Ports of Los Angeles and Beyond*, University of Chicago Press (Chicago, IL), 2023.
8. Susmita Baral, 'Who Controls the Internet? US Government Hands over Control to ICANN', *International Business Times*, 3 October 2016: https://www.ibtimes.com/who-controls-internet-us-government-hands-over-control-icann-2425491.

Text © 2023 John Wiley & Sons Ltd. Images: pp 30–31 © Wendy W Fok and Yarzar Hlaing; pp 32(t), 35(b), 36(t) © Wendy W Fok and Jessica Marquez; pp 32(b), 34, 35(t) © Wendy W Fok and Lucy C Liu; p 36(b) Wendy W Fok, Yvonne Fu and Lin Zhu

Jesse Damiani

Architecture in Postreality

Sabrina Ratté,
Objets—monde,
2022

Much of the rhetoric that defines digital experience emphasises its immateriality and infinitude, notably interfacing with the 'cloud', yet this is predicated on massive physical constructions around the world. Ratté reimagines the material impact of these infrastructures by visualising them as monumental ruins, reflective of their outsized toll on the planet.

Emerging Approaches to Space in Hybrid Realities

For decades, the realm within which architects work was limited to its real-world materiality and ideas of industrialised modernism. This straitjacketed prescription has recently been challenged by the advent of the virtual, through technologies that have blown the profession wide open to new and highly dexterous spatial opportunities that question the old adages that sustained many generations of architects. Curator and writer **Jesse Damiani** reveals some of the ramifications for design.

untitled, xyz, *Monument of Errors*, 2022

Architectural error becomes artistic subject in *Monument of Errors*, foregrounding virtual architecture's affordances in a construction of ordered glitch.

In the 20th century, Western understandings of space exploded in complexity. Landmark developments in physics, including the theory of relativity, quantum mechanics, dark matter and Big Bang cosmology introduced mind-bending new ideas about the structure of the universe. Meanwhile, key developments in architecture, social sciences and other domains of knowledge deconstructed the definition of 'space', expanding its role in reality construction. The aforementioned remain the subject of debate and research today, but in the second half of the 20th century, another set of developments precipitated a major shift, one with more application in everyday life: the advent of virtual space through computing.

Over the ensuing decades, manifestations of virtual space have increased in number, kind and complexity, and now underlie many routine aspects of contemporary life. It is not only that virtual space has asserted its unique affordances relative to the physical, but that the former now pervades the latter in ways large and small. The notion of 'multispace' offers a vital means by which to understand this blurring of reality, conceptualising the contemporary spatial condition as the sum of the physical, digital and the ever-emerging hybridities.

This evolution in the human understanding of space is representative of a broader ontological shift, a reality paradigm I call 'Postreality'.[1] Under Postreality, the role of architects is evolving, as is the language of architecture itself. Recent efforts by architects operating as hybrid practitioners present glimpses of these changes, as do those of artists without formal architectural training, who have also begun to meaningfully engage in architectural endeavours.

From Modernity to Postreality
Postreality can be viewed as the contemporary iteration of reality that emerges from, and in contradistinction to, modernity. This prior reality paradigm was predicated on Enlightenment values and the mechanisms of the Industrial Revolution, and its principal development was the framing of reality as universal and consistent. If modernity can be seen as the first time humans realised a monolithic reality at global scale through the vectors of colonialism and capitalism, Postreality can be seen as deconstructing this hegemony through an emphasis on multiplicity and decentralisation. Though drawing from postmodernist and posthumanist scholarship, Postreality is more fully realised as metamodern and synthetic; in its best expressions, it is bricolage and radical reimagination; at its worst, devolution into cross-talk, disjunction and attention fracture. In Postreality, the virtual is neither hypothetical nor inferior to physical reality: it is a different but equal – and interdependent – dimension of space with unique capacities and constraints.

Under modernity's regime, the role of the architect was circumscribed not only by the material constraints of the physical world but by the sociocultural and philosophical boundaries of the Enlightenment project – which implicitly and explicitly dictate use value in architectural efforts and modes of expression. Two centuries later, as power and wealth continue to aggregate among the elite, architects often find themselves working in a field whose social milieu professes to be progressive but in practice is often necessarily conservative. A tension exists for architects who imagine themselves as mediators between private capital and the public effect of a building – that is, to 'go beyond the brief'. This sense of transcending the design task set out by capital is where, in idealistic imaginings, modern architecture and modern art diverge. The modern artist, assumed to be unhindered by building codes, regulations and clients, is seen as liberated from capital, executing their vision in its raw, untampered essence.

Yet it is more evident than ever that the majority of artists are subordinated by capital. As gaming and metaverse initiatives become commonplace, some artists are gravitating towards them as a means of applying their skills to design spaces in these environments. In architecture, new opportunities and slow job-market growth have sent some architects on unconventional career paths. This social dynamic, coupled with the rising prominence of virtual space in the construction of reality, indicates an emerging milieu that demands new considerations. What possibilities might Postreality offer for generating novel modes of reality creation in an era marked by an increasing convergence between physical and digital space?

The Digital Dimensions of Public Architecture and Data as Material
Untitled, xyz (née Kirk Frankel) is an architect who creates art and architecture for the metaverse. In *Monument of Errors* (2021), Frankel established an Escheresque assemblage of artefacts from the built world: columns, capitals and pedestals jigsawed together, defying conventional usage. The composition, framed by an almost tilt-shift lens depth-of-field, perturbs the eye's expectations of distance and scale. The artist concludes that 'the resulting architecture is a diagram of dead branches, of futures not achieved'.[2] This is not merely a speculative or liquid architecture, nor is it an imbuing of functional space with a provocative narrative thesis, but rather an atomising of the elements of architecture as material, subverting their use value (ie colonnade as structural support versus purely aesthetic entity), and reassembling them into a logic predicated on the infinite and manipulable physics of the virtual.

As a work of art showcased in the 'Elsewhere is a Negative Mirror' exhibition at the Vellum LA art gallery in Los Angeles (2022) and sold as a non-fungible token (NFT), *Monument* also engaged in a dialogue of public versus private, sold to one owner as an artwork but still viewable by all.

Frankel's work with the Museum of Crypto Art's (MoC△) ROOMs project (2022) extended the possibilities for bottom-up social connection and emergence in virtual architecture. In this project, individual architectural spaces designed by the architect-artist, interoperable across any metaverse platform, were sold as ROOM NFTs. Holders of a ROOM NFT are entitled to independently install artworks and experiences per their preference, thus co-creating the public function of a given space. Physical distances collapse – anyone with a working computer can visit these ROOMs.

Experiments with virtuality can also have practical aims towards understanding physical architectures built with, or in response to a robust digital material: data. Astronomer Caleb Scharf has proposed that information is not an inert by-product of human behaviour, but that it is in fact *alive* – that data is an aggregate lifeform with its own needs and desires.[3] Digital technologies create ever new means for this 'dataome' to manifest itself – and for the dataome to be rendered legible to humans.

In a series of prescient early-career works, architect and artist Behnaz Farahi interrogated this relationship between the human body and the 'corpus' of data enmeshing us. In *The Living, Breathing Wall* (2013) and its follow-up *Breathing Wall II* (2014), she created walls that perceive and react to human speech and hand movements, respectively. In so doing, she proposes new valences of 'public' that exist when built environments respond to the bodies moving through them. *Aurora* (2016), a kinetic ceiling that senses and responds to movement below it, raises the stakes beyond interaction, asking what it means for a building to maintain knowledge of specific individuals over time. Though still relatively young, the proliferation of smart Internet of Things devices in the home and in public form a digital architecture of knowledge – about individuals and collective patterns. *Aurora* captures the promise and peril of imbuing virtual approaches in physical space: simultaneously inquisitive about the new modes of knowing that might develop through adaptive architectures and cognisant of the inevitable extraction that will follow. These three works reveal how spatial understandings rooted in the language of data might alter the built environment, prompting ethical questions at the intersections of private and public, intimacy and anonymity, and empowerment and extraction.

Architectural Interventions by Artists

Krista Kim, MadMaraca and Sabrina Ratté are artists whose contributions offer clues to the role that those without conventional pedigrees might offer architecture under Postreality. Kim's *Mars House* (2021) made history as the first 'digital NFT house'. A few months after the initial sale, Kim debuted a version of the house on the platform Spatial, letting users visit the house via mobile, desktop or extended reality (XR) headset. A mental-health advocate, Kim built the house during Covid-enforced quarantine, where she says she 'became inspired to create my vision of a world of meditativeness … of how the practice of meditation can also be integrated into our everyday lives through art, architecture, design and fashion'.[4] The house, constructed of virtual glass and light, invites audiences to experience it as a part of their day, even if only for a few moments. Though the corresponding NFT does grant the owner the right to commission a physical corollary, the 'authentic' expression of *Mars House* is a manifestation of reality on virtual terms – one that, though participating in a market, is intended as a sort of niche public good.

Krista Kim,
Mars House,
2021

right: In its simultaneous expression as art, NFT and architecture, *Mars House* is a multispatial effort with a single goal in mind: helping visitors find a moment of meditation, whether on their own or with others.

Behnaz Farahi,
Aurora,
2016

Could the dynamic architecture of the future not only respond to individuals, but convey information about collective human movement? In asking this question, *Aurora* highlights the ways that data is becoming a potent material in physical construction.

Behnaz Farahi,
Breathing Wall II,
2014

below: The work examines how materials, form and interactive systems of control relate to each other in the creation of 'empathetic' relationships between users and their environment.

Sabrina Ratté,
Undream,
2018

Defying poles of utopia and dystopia, *Undream* suspends viewers in an isolated territory in which the built structure crowns the natural environment in the logic of the digital, blurring notions of land art and virtual architecture.

Sabrina Ratté,
Contre-espace,
Michal and Renata Hornstein
Pavilion for Peace,
Montreal Museum of Fine Arts,
Quebec, Canada,
2022

Physical surface transforms into a portal in this projection on the oldest façade of the museum, through which the artist puts light and stone in negotiation of physical and digital material, with virtual materials manifesting physically through public installation.

Sabrina Ratté examines the relationship between nature, architecture and the digital environment, and how these influence our perception of reality. Many of Ratté's works feature physical-digital cross interpolations, literalising multispace architectures through techniques including photogrammetry, animation, virtual reality (VR) and projection. A homage to Superstudio and the Radical Architecture movement of the 1960s and 1970s, *Undream* (2018) presented an isolated landscape framed by a monumental structure. As the video progresses, the physical impossibilities and unique virtual flourishes become more apparent. As the artist explains, 'the architecture morphs between impossible surfaces and underlying order, interfering with the landscape as it undulates in and out of existence'.[5] In *Monades* (2020), the artist embedded her own body – captured from the physical world using photogrammetry – in a futuristic space, using scale and monumentality to blur sculpture, autobiography and architecture. *Objets-monde* (2022) situated abandoned objects like cars and computer monitors (also captured using photogrammetry) as massive ruins of monumental architecture embedded within their landscapes, in an attempt to represent how the detritus of technology becomes part of the physical world. Digital imagination converged with physicality in *Contre-espace* (2022), a massive projection on a façade of the Montreal Museum of Fine Arts in Quebec, Canada. In this work, Ratté transformed the museum's façade into a window through which the public could witness visions of virtual architectures and impossible landscapes, replete with signifiers of the digital (glitch, noise, etc).

MadMaraca, who also goes by Mari, is an artist whose primary material is the voxel, the building block of virtual worlds understood simply as a cubic 3D 'pixel'. Works from 2021, such as *Emiris, Hidden*

MadMaraca,
Emiris,
2021

Voxel-based architecture, the focus of MadMaraca's practice, applies the language of video games to constructions, and gestures to future technologies that would entail a novel relationship to architectural materials.

Temple and *The Lost City of Eslinas* are of such ornateness and complexity that many viewers only realise they are built with voxels by zooming in on a given image or video. Yet once this becomes apparent, a clear connection emerges to the material and aesthetics of *Minecraft*, the best-selling video game in history, in which participants not only play games, but actually participate in the creation of items, tools and structures, as well as the resulting in-game communities and economies.

With hundreds of millions worldwide participating in the ongoing creation and continuation of this game universe, it is not hard to imagine how voxel-based architectures will feel commonplace as an aesthetic language for many who came of age in the 21st century. By creating artistic voxel-based constructions, MadMaraca engages in a sensemaking exercise for future design and architectural languages. Taking a more speculative angle, the artist's work also offers a prospective vision for a future in which technologies like 3D printing and nanobots enable architects to conceive of projects at the level of the particle, rather than the logistics involved with mined or fabricated components.

Multispatial Fluencies for Postreality

These works share a sense that virtual space and materials are not only real, but capable of fostering novel ontologies in both domains through emergent social constructions. The physical world is bound by spacetime, material limits, societal expectations and other inherited boundaries. Virtual imagination stands in opposition to these constraints, proposing fluid approaches to conceiving, building and populating spaces, while simultaneously pervading the physical in countless ways: map applications that influence navigation patterns, social-media trends that alter how hotels are designed, video-conferencing platforms that transform any space into the workplace. Meanwhile, through search engines and social networks, domains of knowledge diffuse into one another, prompting novel social dynamics that make way for global, hybrid and idiosyncratic practitioners to participate and learn from each other.

Artists and game developers are already encroaching on the spatial domains of architecture, and with the advent of publicly available large multimodal deep-learning models (such as OpenAI's GPT-4 and Google's PaLM-E), the pace of this knowledge blur is likely to accelerate. These changes will not erase the need for architects under Postreality, but they will cast the role as more thoroughly hybrid and multispatial, demanding understanding and application of the types of fluencies in new dimensions being explored by artists such as those discussed here. Through this, architecture might find ways to serve a multispatial public and to reimagine its role as a means of expressing and interpolating reality in a postreal context. Δ

Notes
1. Jesse Damiani, 'Curating in Postreality', Right Click Save, 16 January 2023: https://www.rightclicksave.com/article/curating-in-postreality.
2. Kirk Frankel, *Monument of Errors*, 2022: https://superrare.com/artwork-v2/monument-of-errors-31827.
3. See Caleb Scharf, *The Ascent of Information: Books, Bits, Genes, Machines, and Life's Unending Algorithm*, Riverhead Books (New York), 2021.
4. Alberto Giacometti, 'Mars House by Krista Kim'," Sothebys.com, 2 November 2021: https://www.sothebys.com/en/articles/mars-house-by-krista-kim-on-view-in-new-york.
5. Sabrina Ratté, 'Undream', 2018: https://sabrinaratte.com/UNDREAM-2018.

Text © 2023 John Wiley & Sons Ltd. Images: pp 38–9, 44–5 Courtesy of the artist; p 40 © untitled, xyz; pp 42–3(t) photo Christopher Parsons; pp 42–3(bl) © Krista Kim Studio Inc; p 43(r) photo Ramin Khah; p 45 photo Denis Farley; pp 46–7 © MadMaraca, 2021

Paula Strunden

Touching, Licking, Tasting

Performing Multisensory Spatial Perception Through Extended-Reality Models

```
Paula Strunden,
Rhetorical Bodies,
frei_raum Q21,
   Vienna,
    2022
```

right: Re-examining corporal communication in an age of virtuality allows two immersants to temporarily step away from remote conversations using the familiar two-dimensional audiovisual channels, and instead communicate non-verbally through spatial and temporal effects triggered by their bodily gestures and movements in real time.

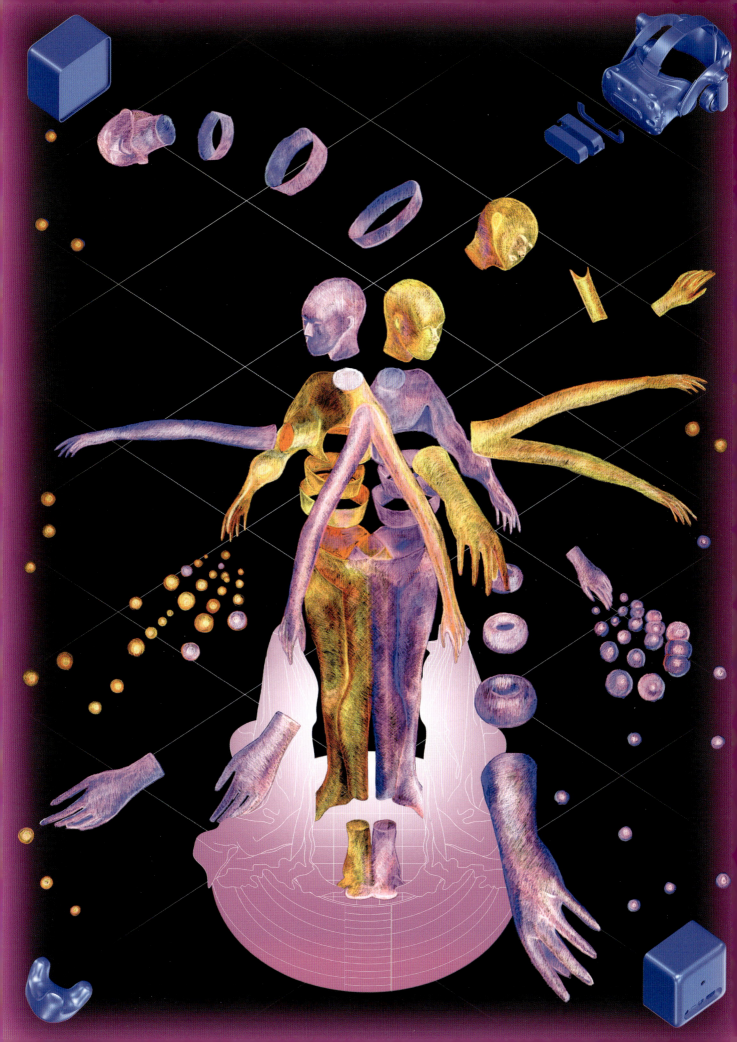

There has been much written speculation about leaving the body on entering fully virtual space. However, it is clear that the only reason we can experience virtual reality is precisely because we are embodied. Transdisciplinary researcher and architectural artist **Paula Strunden** works at the intersection of the real and the virtual, exploiting our body's important conduits for complete sensory and visceral experience of augmented space.

Thirty years ago, the architectural theorist Karen A Franck posed the crucial question: 'When I enter Virtual Reality, What Body Will I Leave behind?'.[1] Franck's essay, published in the *D Architects in Cyberspace* special issue in 1995, begins with a detailed account of how it feels to place a virtual-reality (VR) headset on her head, slip a pair of gloves over her fingers, put on a motion-capture suit, take a first step and reach into virtual space. She describes acting in virtual space and interacting with virtual objects as an inherently physical undertaking that needs her 'eyes and ears to do the seeing and hearing; my arms, hands, legs and feet ... to do the moving'.[2] It is not the physical body that is left behind, she explains, as 'without it, I am in no world at all'.[3] Instead, it is her body's capacity to interact, respond and attune to a new environment with different sets of laws that enables her to experience alternative ways of 'being-in-the-world'.

In the same vein, in 1996 the literary critic Nancy Katherine Hayles proclaimed: 'If ... we can see, hear, feel, and interact with virtual worlds only because we are embodied, why is there so much noise about the perception of cyberspace as a disembodied medium?'[4] Three decades later, the noise still persists, and the false premise of escaping, overcoming and transcending our physical bodies continues to be fuelled by the military, gaming and pornography industries that have significantly contributed to the technological development. While valuable insights by early pioneers in the field are being eclipsed, video-game designer and researcher Brenda Laurel lamented in a 2018 interview: 'What frustrates me most is that we learned some shit that some people aren't paying attention to,' and that today's practitioners are 'probably not even aware of what was built in the early '90s, mostly by women.'[5]

Dissolving Boundaries
During the first wave of VR, numerous female artists and theorists explored the relationship between virtual technologies and physical bodies, placing them at the core of their experimental configurations. Seminal works, such as Brenda Laurel's and Rachel Strickland's *Placeholder* (1993), Char Davies' *Osmose* (1995) and Catherine Richards' *Spectral Bodies* (2000),[6] challenged prevailing assumptions that virtual technologies are disembodied media. They developed techniques to navigate virtual worlds intuitively, control their environment through natural interfaces such as touch, breath or balance, and interact simultaneously via different sensory modalities. These artists laid the groundwork for transcending the boundaries of binary thinking in the realm of human-computer interaction, and re-interweave the dualities of actual/virtual, mind/body, subjective/objective and theory/practice.

```
Char Davies,
Vertical Tree,
Osmose,
1995
```

Digital still captured in real time through a head-mounted display (HMD) during a live performance of an immersive virtual environment, *Osmose*.

In the early 1990s, Douglas MacLeod, the director of the Canadian Art and Virtual Environments Project, recalled that the term 'virtual reality' was filled with overblown media hype and negative associations with violent video games, and as a result decided to characterise the groundbreaking artistic explorations they facilitated as 'three-dimensional, interactive and real-time'.[7] His foresight corresponds with the persistent need to develop a shared vocabulary for a new perceptual framework that allows architects and artists to move beyond purely technical considerations and unveil new ways of experiencing hybrid spatialities through interdisciplinary and extended spatial practices.

While virtual technologies and head-mounted displays are increasingly being adopted in architectural research and practice, the understanding of the technology falsely resides within the representational logic of ocular-centric perspectival renderings, bending two-dimensional visuals around immobile heads. Yet, the core of virtual technologies – independent of whether we access it through virtual-, augmented- or mixed-reality goggles – is an embodied form of spatial and object-based computing, enabling real-time interaction with digital information in the real world. This raises the pertinent question: How does the transformation of surrounding objects and spaces into interfaces, and the reconfiguration of bodies into input devices, affect our concept of self, our boundaries to things and our relational dynamics to the built environment?

Constructing Realities

To speculate upon this question, I developed a hybrid way of working that intersects architectural design methods with real-time techniques and user-oriented practices from the fields of scenography, performance and game design. Building on Thea Brejzek's and Lawrence Wallen's concept of the 'autonomous model',[8] I build full-scale responsive and full-body immersive installations that I refer to as performative 1:1 extended-reality models (XRMs). These combine virtual technologies with physical objects and spaces, and respond to the user's behaviour by merging the visual and auditory feedback of virtual devices with kinaesthetic, tactile, olfactory and gustatory stimuli of material artefacts, enabling the users to explore the whole multisensory spectrum of hybrid spatial experiences. Rather than focusing on the hardware and software employed to design and develop these models, the emphasis is placed on the subjective experience of the individuals interacting with the models, which in return are perceived as an independently acting entity, a reality in themselves.[9]

To highlight the various sensory impacts and emotional effects of lived experiences, I borrow the term 'immersant', coined by Char Davies, who empathetically foregrounds the importance of engaging with, caring for and attending to the environment immersed in through natural and intuitive interactions.[10] The active engagement and emotional involvement within the virtual world positively correlates with the diminished perception of it as an artificial construct and the increased perception of it as personally significant and, thus, real.[11] Lived experience is understood here from a phenomenological perspective as a highly subjective embodied, embedded, enacted and extended perceptual dimension and active practice of knowing. Once immersants realise that they can physically experience virtual effects and effectively control, shape and influence their behaviour as well as their surrounding environment, cognitive processes that unveil the depth of architectural relations between body/mind/psyche are set in motion, opening up a whole new field of research, native to the medium.

By exposing my body to a moment in time and space where the actual and virtual converge, a simultaneous sense of presence can be experienced in the 'here' and 'there', characterised by a dynamic, continuously shifting nature as opposed to a static and stable state. This process of entanglement involves delving into an open-ended trajectory of art-based research and design fiction, and culminated in the conception and exhibition of three prototypical case studies, publicly tested between 2021 and 2023.[12]

Paula Strunden,
Infra-thin Magick,
Exhibit Gallery,
Academy of Fine Arts Vienna,
2022

left: The ceremony mistress guides the immersant through the 15- to 20-minute-long initiation ritual by lowering one after the other infra-thin objects from the ceiling while being present in virtual space as a flying, hopping or grooming raven, depending on her movements in real time.

below: The moment the immersant touches and lifts the infra-thin object no 3 Seeing Orb, her eyes are moved inside the volume held in between her hands, allowing her to control her vision and explore its relation to balance, gravity and touch by carefully repositioning the object at hand.

opposite, top left: Preliminary insights are gathered from over 150 *Infra-thin Magick* reflection cards that immersants filled out after having taken part in the initiation ritual and having been introduced to the space in the liminal, the gap between physical and virtual reality.

In *Rhetorical Bodies*, two immersants use tracked wearables to communicate non-verbally through bodily gestures and movements, reconfiguring the positioning of their body parts relative to themselves and each other. This immersive experience allows two people to step inside each other's bodies, modifying and synchronising movements in real time, such as seeing with their feet, walking through their balance or touching with their eyes, revealing the inherent ambiguity and dynamic plasticity of bodily boundaries.

In *Infra-thin Magick*, one immersant is initiated through a series of ceremonial practices to the realm that unfolds where material and virtual space intersect. Through eating, drinking, dancing and chanting, the immersant connects with three different artefacts that respond unexpectedly to their movements and senses. Through these unanticipated interactions, the ceremony mistress, equally present physically and virtually, challenges the immersants to question the taken-for-granted features of things, as well as the presupposed observer-observed boundary, leading to an instinctual feeling that the objects encountered have their own agency.

In *Alison's Room*, a speaking cat guides one immersant through a spatio-temporal reconstruction of Alison Smithson's working room and archive. Handling the room's furniture elements, the immersant intuitively navigates within a few square metres between six distinct architectural projects by the Smithsons. By controlling the order, length and type of space they inhabit, immersants generate their own unique multidimensional archival reconstruction

of Alison's Room, forging an intimate connection with their environment, triggering associative thoughts, and potentially gaining novel insights into the Smithsons' work.

Together, these three models explore spatial perception in extended-reality through the lens of our bodies, the objects we interact with, and the spaces we are immersed in. While equally present within one another, the changing lenses reset the focus on different sensory modalities, unveiling the interplay among the actants and forces that reveal themselves once the XRM starts its game.

Imagining Futures

As human-computer interaction infiltrates our surrounding objects and spaces, it becomes increasingly apparent that we need to seek out extended tools that enable us to directly experience, explore and speculate upon what it means to inhabit, interconnect and interact within hybrid spatial environments. While most of the knowledge regarding multimodal spatial perception resides deep in our unconsciousness, the XRM helps us reveal embodied cognitive processes we have previously taken for granted, and surface otherwise unconsciously experienced relations between bodies, objects and spaces through this newly emerging realm. The XRM has the potential to function as an active agent in the co-creation and dissemination of architectural knowledge, as it liquifies the boundaries among all participating actors and renders the dissolution of the actual/virtual dichotomies experienceable. In the same vein that feminist and new materialist discourses have developed analytical tools and theoretical frameworks to describe the interconnectedness and interdependence of different parts within a given system, such as Jane Bennett's 'vitality of things'[13] or Karen Barad's 'agential realism',[14] it becomes necessary to design, build and test experiential and performative models of potential non-hierarchical and non-binary futures that 'act as catalysts for public debate and discussion about the kinds of futures people really want'.[15]

Nevertheless, even if the XRM reconfigures bodies, objects and spaces in an active feedback loop, in which they become mutually responsible for one another as 'co-producer of reality',[16] they will remain in a reality that is constructed and coded by humans, that is embedded and embodied in human thought and its understanding of the world. Although the XRM has the capacity to question the 'Cartesian presupposition that there is an inherent boundary between observer and observed, knower and known',[17] Char Davies claimed, using the example of the simulated bird, that all it 'can ever be is the sum of our (very limited) knowledge

Paula Strunden,
Rhetorical Bodies,
MU Hybrid Art House,
Eindhoven,
The Netherlands,
2023

This networked XR experience allows two immersants to communicate through gestures, motions and dance, translating their movements into sounds and transforming their physical forms into interactive embodied synthesisers.

Paula Strunden,
Alison's Room,
Nieuwe Instituut,
Rotterdam, 2022

above: Set-up of the performative 1:1 extended-reality model (XRM) of Alison Smithson's workspace and archive. The model is virtually overlaid with six distinct architectural projects by the Smithsons that immersants can inhabit via a VR headset: sitting on the chair, taking a folder from the shelf, looking outside the window or petting the cat.

right: Once the immersant touches the *Little Garden of Paradise* (c 1410) painting by Upper Rheinish Masters positioned on the mantelpiece of the archive room, the wall opens up and exposes a garden that can be entered through the chimney. Having crawled inside, the immersant can pick apples or play the harp, which takes them to the Smithson's House of the Future, referencing the medieval painting.

far right: The tracked cat, Sarafina, can be pulled around by the invigilator, intuitively guiding the immersant's attention and movement through the multidimensional spatio-temporal experience. It purrs upon being touched, and provides a deep level of trust and familiarity within the newly behaving spatial dimension.

It is high time for spatial and multisensory designers to participate in shaping the future of ubiquitous computing

below: Conceptual hand-drawing of Alison Smithson's working room and archive based on colour photography of the space taken by Sandra Lousada in 2003, before the material collection was split between the Frances Loeb Library at Harvard University in Cambridge, Massachusetts, the Nieuwe Instituut in Rotterdam and the private Smithson Family Collection in London.

about birds – it has no "otherness", no mysterious being, no autonomous life'.[18] Her concern that one day 'our culture may consider the simulated bird (that obeys our command) to be enough and perhaps even superior to the real entity' anticipates the danger of depriving ourselves of the intrinsic value of other life forms and replacing them with virtual representations that reflect our limited viewpoints.[19] Davies warned that as a result we could become blind to environmental degradation as we create a world that is detached from physical reality and lacks a sense of reverence.

To move towards a more holistic and sustainable future that values the autonomy of 'other' things, it is crucial to counteract the narrative of virtual technologies as a disembodied medium for escaping the material world. It is high time for spatial and multisensory designers to participate in shaping the future of ubiquitous computing, and for the extended-reality industries to invest in the past, present and future of artistic and designerly explorations in embodied virtuality. ⌀

Notes

1. Karen A Franck, 'When I Enter Virtual Reality, What Body Will I Leave Behind?', in Martin Pearce and Neil Spiller (eds), ⌀ *Architects in Cyberspace,* no 118, 1995, pp 20–24.
2. *Ibid*, p 20.
3. *Ibid*.
4. Katherine N Hayles, 'Embodied Virtuality: Or How to Put the Body Back into the Picture', in Douglas MacLeod and Mary Anne Moser (eds), *Immersed in Technology: Art and Virtual Environments*, MIT Press (Cambridge, MA), 1996, p 1.
5. Claire L Evans, 'Brenda Laurel's Placeholder: In Dreams Everybody Flies Their Own Way', Artlink, 1 December 2018: https://www.artlink.com.au/articles/4724/brenda-laurelE28099s-placeholder-in-dreams-everybody-fl/.
6. Brenda Laurel and Rachel Strickland, *Placehoder*, 1993: https://vimeo.com/27344103; Char Davies, *Osmose*, 1995: https://www.youtube.com/watch?v=54O4VP3tCoY; Catherine Richards, *Spectral Bodies*, 2000: http://www.catherinerichards.ca/artwork2/Spectral-index.html.
7. Douglas MacLeod and Mary Anne Moser (eds), *Immersed in Technology: Art and Virtual Environments*, MIT Press (Cambridge, MA), 1996, pp x–xiii.
8. Thea Brejzek and Lawrence Wallen, *The Model as Performance: Staging Space in Theatre and Architecture*, Bloomsbury (London), 2017, p 2.
9. Olafur Eliasson, 'Models are Real', in *Models*, vol 306090, Princeton Architectural Press (New York), 2007, p 19.
10. Char Davies, 'Osmose: Notes on Being in Immersive Virtual Space', in Colin Beardon and Lone Malmborg (eds), *Digital Creativity: A Reader*, Swets & Zeitlinger Publishers (Lisse), 2002, pp 101–10.
11. Oliver Grau, *Virtuelle Kunst in der Geschichte und Gegenwart*, Dietrich Reimer (Berlin), 2000, p 193.
12. These studies form the backbone of my PhD research, conducted under the supervision of Angelika Schnell at the Academy of Fine Arts Vienna, as part of 'Communities of Tacit Knowledge (TACK): Architecture and its Ways of Knowing' funded by the European Union's Horizon 2020 research and innovation programme under the Marie Skłodowska-Curie grant agreement No 860413. They have been publicly exhibited in the following: 'No Dancing Allowed', curated by Bogomir Doringer, frei_raum Q21, Vienna, 22 June to 20 November 2022 and 'Hybrid Tales for Hybrid Times' curated by Angelique Spaninks, MU Hybrid Art House, Eindhoven, 6 July to 26 August 2023; 'Speculative Fiction', curated by Stephanie Damianitsch, Exhibit Gallery, Academy of Fine Arts Vienna, 9 July to 16 October 2022; 'Virtual CIAM Museum', curated by Dirk van den Heuvel, Nieuwe Instituut, Rotterdam, 24 November 2022 to 8 January 2023.
13. Jane Bennett, *Vibrant Matter: A Political Ecology of Things*, Duke University Press (Durham, NC), 2010.
14. Karen Barad, *Meeting the Universe Halfway: Quantum Physics and the Entanglement of Matter and Meaning*, Duke University Press (Durham, NC), 2007.
15. Anthony Dunne and Fiona Raby, *Speculative Everything: Design, Fiction, and Social Dreaming*, MIT Press (Cambridge, MA), 2013, p 6.
16. Eliasson, *op cit*, p 19.
17. Barad, *op cit*, p 154.
18. Char Davies *et al*, 'Natural Artifice', in Mary Ann Moser (ed), *The Bioapparatus*, Banff Centre for the Arts (Banff), 1991, p 16.
19. *Ibid*.

Text © 2023 John Wiley & Sons Ltd. Images: pp 49, 53(b), 55 © Paula Strunden, 2022; p 51 © Char Davies; p 52 © Maria Belova, 2022; pp 53(t), 54 © Riccardo De Vecchi, 2022

Holly Nielsen

Space Popular (Lara Lesmes and Fredrik Hellberg), 'The Venn Room', Estonian Museum of Architecture, Tallinn Architecture Biennale (TAB), Tallinn, Estonia, 2019

This installation and virtual-reality (VR) film helped visitors to visualise how multifaceted their domestic environments are. Through this medium the creators showed how we co-create and embody our spaces, the kitchen table being a central site.

MULTIPURPOSE DOMESTICITY

LABOUR, LEISURE AND KITCHEN TABLES

In the grip of the viral contagion of the recent past and its attendant lockdowns, many of us started working from home for the first time and transitioning to various online communication methods such as Zoom or Teams. However, home working is not a new phenomenon; our domestic spaces have always had to embrace and adapt to multifunctional activities they may not have been designed for. The introduction of online spaces, though, adds a new layer to consider. Historian and writer **Holly Nielsen** explores our contemporary domestic condition, its histories and its interaction with electronic space.

Through the multiple lockdowns as a result of the Covid-19 pandemic, many of us have been confronted with our domestic space having to subsume roles and uses that previously may have been unfamiliar to us. However, domestic space being multipurpose is not a new development. There is a longer history of multipurpose domesticity with which to give context to this seemingly new phenomenon. The complex nature of what even constitutes domesticity, the emotionally loaded word of 'home' and the mixture of daily rituals and more ephemeral actions that take place in the domestic realm make its analysis complex. Work, leisure and socialisation all occur within the same space, overlapping one another. The introduction of the digital complicates this further, requiring us not to separate the digital and the analogue, but to see them as a blending of space, each influencing and impacting the other. Through this understanding, we can situate contemporary experiences of multipurpose domesticity within these longer histories.

Historical Understandings of Domestic Space

Understandings of the home as a multipurpose space have often been framed through the lens of the family, with many historians and researchers looking at how the class differences in housing impacted relations to this space. The environmental psychologist Roger Hart studied how children growing up in a small town in Vermont experience their world in his work *Children's Experience of Place* (1979), arguing that, while working-class homes may have had less physical space, the child may have more freedom as their play was not expected to be restricted to rooms with that express purpose.[1] Historian John Gillis emphasises both space and time as important axes for family practices, both internal and within broader social

Old illustration of a family meal in an Alsatian farmhouse, published in *L'Illustration Journal Universel*, Paris, 1857

Kitchen tables were a site of family politics, and highlighted gender roles and categories of age. This was particularly apparent during mealtimes.

contexts. He argues that, within the wider metaphors of the home, families produced symbolically loaded places such as the back door and the parlour.[2] Historians such as Megan Doolittle and Julie-Marie Strange have developed upon Gillis's notion of symbolically loaded places within the domestic setting by exploring the shifting meanings of the material culture of the British working-class home. In particular, they explore the relation of the material to family dynamics via a focus on the father's chair.[3]

By using domestic material culture, we can highlight the fluidity and diversity of domestic space through everyday activities and items. Julie-Marie Strange has examined the kitchen table through understanding teatime as a ritual of family togetherness which helped locate men at the core of British household space, while noting that the kitchen table in the working-class home was a multipurpose space. She observes that even affluent working-class families lived overwhelmingly in one room, making the literally named 'living room' the main site of family space,[4] which as a result saw numerous uses, including eating, leisure, children's play and relaxation. An essential part of this space was the table. As Strange writes: 'Tables in working-class homes, whether circular or square, were modest in size, frequently multi-purpose and facilitated physical proximity between seated family members, chairs permitting, facing each other in convivial arrangement.'[5] Not all tables were a permanent fixture; some were instead brought out to facilitate food consumption or family togetherness. While the primary use of the table may have been at mealtimes, it was a multipurpose site and could also serve for play, socialisation and labour within late 19th- and early 20th-century working-class homes.

A Longer History of Working from Home

The Covid-19 pandemic precipitated a heightened awareness and indeed practice of the domestic as multipurpose. In my own life, I first began researching and writing about multipurpose domesticity from a historical perspective during the first lockdown, working at a kitchen table around which three of us congregated every day. Huge numbers of people were facing their living space having to be their sole place of rest, work, socialisation (even if largely digital or with those living in the same household), as well as the place of daily living routines. Of course, this change for many was not felt equally. Socioeconomics, geographic location, gender dynamics, along with any number of vectors, influenced the experience. Undoubtedly, though, many of us were now having to use our domestic spaces in ways and at times that were new to us.

In Britain, at least, this was nothing new. Tailoring, sewing, keeping small shops and washing, among many forms of both seasonal and permanent waged labour, have taken place in and around the home for centuries. However, as a consequence of the often gendered nature of working from home and the difficulty in tracking and gaining reliable data on it because of its seasonal and more ephemeral nature – occurring as it does around other rhythms of daily home life – this home-based work is more often overlooked compared to other forms of labour.

Helen McCarthy has highlighted the role of waged labour taking place in the home by British women in the 19th and 20th centuries.[6] As the Industrial Revolution hit and an increasing amount of work was brought out of homes and into factories, this type of home-based waged labour did not disappear, but developed alongside the modern factory system, with working-class mothers playing a major part due to childcare demands.

A family watching television in their living room, 1948

The introduction of entertainment technology to the home added another layer to spaces, whether it was through the soundscapes of the radio and wireless, or images from the television or computer screen.

59

Screenshot of *Mystery House* running on Apple II, 1980

Game developer Roberta Williams created perhaps the first depiction of a domestic setting in a digital game. Through its development, *Mystery House* highlights the home both as a site of work and as an imagined space within the game itself.

Although digital and online spaces are accessed via hardware, to look at these digital spaces as entirely separate from physical space only tells part of the story

Space Popular (Lara Lesmes and Fredrik Hellberg), 'The Venn Room', Estonian Museum of Architecture, Tallinn Architecture Biennale (TAB), Tallinn, Estonia, 2019

Through clashing yet familiar images, the creators of this installation and VR film helped to visually represent the multipurpose nature of domesticity.

Looking at a more recent example, Laine Nooney has written about the California-based game designer Roberta Williams who designed potentially one of the first video games with a domestic setting – *Mystery House*, released in 1980 – at her kitchen table, which allowed for her to work on the design while keeping an eye on her children. As Nooney puts it, 'perhaps Roberta did not come to the table so much as the table came to her, as an object with agency within a broader condensation of domestic, architectural, and gendered expectations for behaviour and orientation'.[7]

In amongst all of this is the added layer of the digital. Designers and artists have found the layering of the domestic a fruitful space for examination. Space Popular – a research-driven architecture, design and media studio – has used virtual reality, art and installations to explore many of these ideas. Their exhibition 'The Venn Room' at the Tallinn Architecture Biennale (TAB) in 2019 explored these ideas, including screens being portals that both transport and transform the space around them. Although digital and online spaces are accessed via hardware, to look at these digital spaces as entirely separate from physical space only tells part of the story.

White bookshelf, with books arranged by colour

During the Covid-19 lockdowns, the use of Zoom and video calling led more of us to be conscious of the presentation of our domestic space, as the background of our homes also became how we presented ourselves professionally – even if just for the narrow lens of webcam.

People bring themselves, their backgrounds and their surroundings to digital engagement. Conversely, the digital can impact the physical spaces around us. By using digital methods of socialisation, a kitchen table, a bed or any domestic area can be transformed into a space for the type of social interaction that without the digital would not be feasible, with consequent impacts on how we might arrange the space – for example, tidying or decorating spaces with the thought of them being our new Zoom background, and thus our presentation to the world, in mind.

Layers of Domesticity: the Google Docs Party
A contemporary case study which combines both a presence in the multipurpose domestic realm and the utilisation of the domestic in the digital is the 'Google Docs party' thrown on 2 May 2020 by Marie Foulston, a curator and creative director based in the UK. During a lockdown in 2020, Foulston had moved in with her mother and, like so many, was struggling with a lack of socialisation and reduction in space, and how interaction online had become formalised and draining. As she says in her online write-up of the party, 'Where is the space for the mundane, the idle, and the liminal … those subtle and nuanced moments that also come with being together?'[8]

Guests were invited to the party by a link shared in private chat groups, direct messages on social media and emails. Party guests would enter the Google Doc as anonymous animals randomly assigned to them by the Google Docs platform and communicate via writing and interacting with the cells on the public document. Critically, the party involved no voice chat and no communal chat log. Instead, the doc was organised into 'rooms' featured on different pages. The opening page was 'the front door'.

'I tried a lot of doors. The door page was important, as was the coat room tab. I wanted to give just enough of a context for people to respond to, constraints to creatively bounce off and not feel stressed out by a big white page,' Foulston explains.[9] A lot of thought went into the door picture that was chosen to welcome the partygoers. 'I wanted comfort and when I finally found a kind of grey rainy British looking door with two sad looking balloons it felt reassuring and comforting. … I guess it was an odd combination of escapism and humour. Or just a more honest realisation of escapism that doesn't have to be glamorous or exotic, but just comforting.'[10]

Apart from occasionally getting up to get a drink, Foulston was sitting on her bed for the entirety of the party (which ran from about 9pm to midnight). The party was experienced by people from their own domestic setting, but domesticity and familiarity were still escapism. As well as 'the front door' and 'the coat room', one of the tabs was labelled as 'Kitchen'. This helped continue the domestic theming of the space and spoke to the emulation of the mundane yet escapist humour that informed the party. It allowed a layering of a different kind of domesticity on top of background domesticity. It was transformational of the real-world domestic by accessing socialisation that at that point was not possible without the aid of the digital. Real-world domesticity influenced the digital, and in turn, the digital influenced the real world.

Several guests, as well as Foulston herself, remarked that while attending the party, alongside enjoying the experience, they also felt FOMO (fear of missing out) in regards to what was going on in other pages. Like how someone may feel at a party when wondering about what is happening in the other rooms of the house. It became clear that while the Google Docs party was providing a kind of low-key social interaction that other online social interactions may not help to facilitate, it also emulated social anxiety that one may feel at a physical party. To someone observing Foulston as she engaged with the party, by her own admission, they would have seen someone sat on their bed frowning at a screen. As she points out, 'I think this idea that just because something doesn't look "fulfilling" to an external viewer is something we need to culturally interrogate. If I'm sat looking at a screen with a face like a resting moody face does not mean I am doing something that doesn't have value, meaning or can be positive.'[11]

Situating Multipurpose Domesticity

As discussions around working from home and the role of our domestic spaces in our lives become more prevalent due to the experience of lockdowns, it is important to remember the longer histories of multipurpose domesticity. What these spaces are to us and what we use them for is ever changing. By utilising the material culture of the home, we can access the shifting meanings and roles the spaces provide and facilitate and understand how historically as well as presently, multipurpose domesticity is informed by several axes including, but not limited to, socioeconomic, geographic and gender. The added layer of the digital not only highlights this but helps to blur the boundaries of our domestic spaces even further. Our homes have always been multipurpose; the introduction of digital devices is not the beginning of the phenomenon, but another thread to a tapestry of domestic use and analysis. ⌂

Notes
1. Roger Hart, *Children's Experience of Place*, Irvington Publishers (New York), 1979.
2. John R Gillis, *A World of Their Own Making: Myth, Ritual, and the Quest for Family Values*, Harvard University Press (Cambridge, MA), 1996, pp 120–29.
3. Megan Doolittle, 'Time, Space, and Memories: The Father's Chair and Grandfather Clocks in Victorian Working-class Domestic Lives', *Home Cultures*, 8 (3), April 2015, pp 245–64, and Julie-Marie Strange, *Fatherhood and the British Working Class, 1865–1914*, Cambridge University Press (Cambridge), 2015, pp 82–110.
4. Strange, *op cit*, p 86.
5. *Ibid*.
6. Helen McCarthy, *Double Lives: A History of Working Motherhood*, Bloomsbury (London), 2020, pp 44–66.
7. Laine Nooney, 'A Pedestal, A Table, A Love Letter: Archaeologies of Gender in Videogame History', *Game Studies: The International Journal of Computer Game Research,* 13 (2), December 2013: https://gamestudies.org/1302/articles/nooney.
8. Marie Foulston, 'Party in a Shared Google Doc', 13 May 2020: https://onezero.medium.com/party-in-a-shared-google-doc-d576c565706e.
9. Email interview with the author, 22 February 2023.
10. *Ibid*.
11. *Ibid*.

The 'Front door' of Marie Foulston's Google Doc Party, May 2020

This set of rules greeted guests for Foulston's Google Doc Party, organised during a Covid lockdown. The list blends both the acknowledgement of the imagined domestic setting and the realities of the online doc.

Text © 2023 John Wiley & Sons Ltd. Images: pp 56–7, 60 © Space Popular; p 58 © Marzolino/Shutterstock; p 59 © H. Armstrong Roberts/ClassicStock/Getty Images; p 62 © MagicBones/Shutterstock; p 63 © Marie Foulston

Giacomo Pala

CONJUNCTIONS

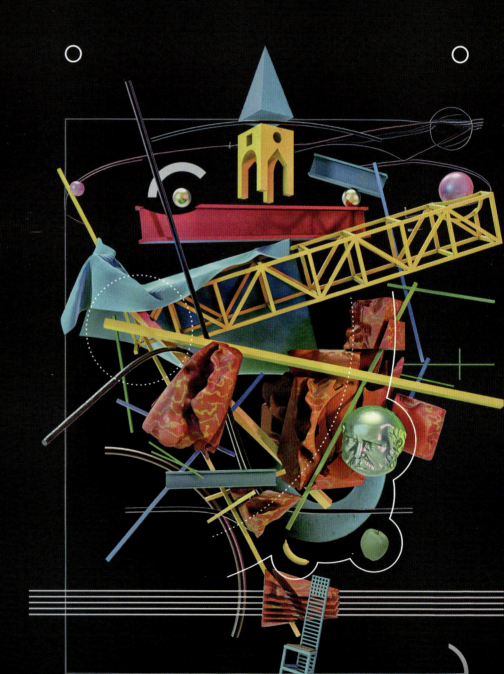

Giacomo Pala,
Conjunction #4,
2023

Architectural composition: domesticity, structures and narratives as a representation of the opening of a domestic realm towards its outside.

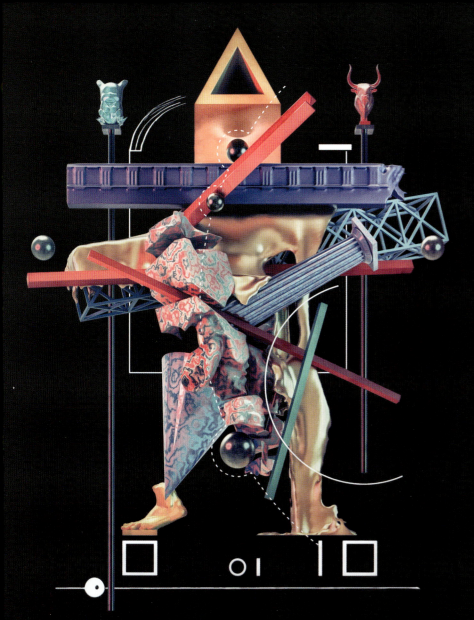

Giacomo Pala,
Conjunction #3,
2023

Architectural composition: history, structures and symbols coming together, defining a space as a conjunction of different times and myths.

OR, SPACE AS OXYMORON

Traditional architectural thought and practice decrees that buildings should be spatially homogeneous, revealing themselves to their viewers and users as episodic and carefully orchestrated wholes. Giacomo Pala argues that the world is more complex than this, and that the digital has further enhanced its heterogeneous festival of formal, semiotic and spatial jump-cutting to establish conjunctions from which we can be architecturally inspired.

Architecture's theories and histories have conditioned us to view space as a locus. Since the ordering of materials and forms defines a representation of memories and a validation of practices, then space is usually seen as a site for action, meaning or contemplation. This myth has been criticised, overturned, invoked, rediscovered, forgotten and re-evaluated throughout the decades: junkspace and the return of utopia; nostalgia and futurism; social awareness and sheer fantasy. Postmodern, neomodern, metamodern, anti-modern and hypermodern spaces have alternatively offered a substitute, a critique and a rediscovery.

Like obsessive teenagers who fall in love too easily, architects and designers must constantly reinvent and rediscover something, while expressing themselves: a new space and the rediscovery of traditions; the new Bauhaus and its criticism. We love the avant-garde one day and despise it the next, only to constantly rediscover that it has never been what we thought it was. The urge to establish one's ego, however, is the sublimation of a failure. The myth of creative genius, stronger than ever as a result of the endless attempts to overcome it (each one still an affirmation of individual prodigy) is inevitable if one wants to design.

Bangkok,
Thailand,
2020

An urban conjunction: an aggregation of infrastructure and nature unfolding as a result of a meticulous layering process driven by symmetrical control.

Vatican Museums,
Rome, Italy,
2022

A 'Toilet' sign in Raphael's room designed in Renaissance style, merging the most mundane needs with Raphael's art.

Nevertheless, it must be acknowledged that the notion of space as a project is not enough, while being an essential prerequisite for design. The world is much too complex to be controlled, programmed, standardised or rather quashed. Beyond the potential violence of any 'plan', there are objects, differences and unexpected oddities. There are entities, uses and qualities evading the architect's and the artist's will, but they define the features of spaces: the intersection of built environment and nature; unexpected uses of objects; the intersection of virtual and material realms; or a 'Toilet' sign designed in Renaissance style within the Vatican Museums rooms are amongst the truest attributes of places.

These and many other qualities convey imageries and memories. They communicate common sentiment and unspoken needs while establishing a conjunction between diversities.

It is not just a matter of admitting that 'creating modern architecture for the twentieth century was a mistake',[1] of contesting the 'notion of unified, coherent architectural form'[2] or of realising that the city is defined on a 'heritage of conflict',[3] but also of recognising that space – as such – has always been indeterminate, at the very least since 'architecture' was invented. Triumphal arches, stairs, escalators, meeting areas filled with USB ports and power outlets, plants, temples, doors and bridges generate deep conjunctions between differences, giving sense to an unpredictable reality.

Public/Private Conjunctions

Conjunctions happen at any scale. A building-spanning freeway in Osaka embodies the conjunction of objects and infrastructures, one of the characterising elements of urban spaces. However one may want to name it, any space is a more or less complex interplay of different purposes, uses and needs. Public space, once defined as the place 'where freedom can unfold its charms and become a visible, tangible reality',[4] takes on new dimensions in the conjunction of public and private. We take part in a new way of living the city, best described by Andrés Jaque while studying the influence of apps such as Grindr on our way of experiencing urban environments: 'a multiplying type of space where simultaneous techno-human settings can be promoted'.[5] Go there with an Uber; commute with Flixbus, Megabus or Neeta Travels; reach yet another exotic destination with EasyJet, Frontier Airlines or 9Air; have a hook-up in an Airbnb and share it on OnlyFans. Move hungry, move foolish.

Local/Global Conjunctions

Conjunctions define a Gordian knot of contradicting traditions. A Chinese entrance to a mediocre alpine architecture in Seefeld in Tirol, Austria, marks the conjunction of the 'global' with the 'local', proving that the latter is nothing but the consequence of the former: 'its residue, its secretion'.[6] Authenticity and identity are suddenly exposed as heirs to a commercial fantasy conceived in the commodification of inflated ideals. The 'local' and the 'global', the 'traditional' and the 'shock of the new' find unexpected conjunctions, taking multiple forms: regional modernities, regionalisms, and even apparently fake settings – from a Chinese Paris to fireplaces re-created by streaming YouTube videos inside televisions, now simulacra of what Gottfried Semper defined as one of the first signs of 'human settlement'.[7]

Osaka, Japan, 2019

A conjunction between infrastructure and buildings: a physical manifestation of the interconnection between objects and infrastructures that defines any city.

Domestic Conjunctions

Conjunctions characterise all spaces we inhabit, including any domestic realm. From the computer one uses to play a video game, to the spaces for the very experience of domestic boredom, space is based on an infinite number of concurrences, not least because everything is dependent on the extraction of the raw materials and minerals that constitute the cosmos, itself 'studded with galaxies and fifteen billion years in the making'.[8] Space expands from the inside out, but in a far different manner than architectural history lectures and design studios have taught us. We dwell in a new kind of phenomenology: a home is not a house, and a home is not a place. It may actually be an unprecedented conjunction of interconnected individualities, each one escaping its own domestication and its physical household. It may be violence, or it may be perversion. It could be a rave on Zoom, gaming, networking, entertainment, excitement, boredom, joy, diversion, hate or love. There are endless encounters of singularities defining new spaces and places for communities: new households made of cables, connections, objects, toys and data.

Today's space is seamlessly built upon juxtapositions and dislocations: conflicts between identities and new fluidities add to the rethinking of predefined categories, uses and imageries. We live within a new and wide ecology, enabling 'the thinking of home, and hence world (*oikos* plus *logos*)'.[9] But this ecology is an eccentric hybrid of known and unknown, familiar and uncanny, liberation and repression. We live within an infrastructural ordering of nature and a naturalisation of technology that has led to an inevitable subjunctivisation of our world-making abilities, creating new kinds of struggles. On the one side there are those who aim to define spaces for sharing experiences and knowledge on a global scale. On the other, there are those who define new power structures through the control and monetisation of different forms of sociality. From within such new global domestic policy, it would be all too easy to believe in a Promethean utopia liberating humanity thanks to techno-sciences, just as it would be quite simplistic to believe the opposite. We should dare saying that we enjoy living in this new world. We love, use and even fetishise bricks, burgers, quinoa, books, prompts, avocados, PDFs, gyms, streaming services, landscapes, bed and breakfasts, and the many more things that make up this new world. There are no saints anymore. Each of us, to some extent, is a sinner. One can sublimate pain by posting severe memes on social media, maybe while eating some authentic pho in Buenos Aires, or some asado in Hanoi. Nevertheless, we all worship the heterogeneous, 'hybrid-', 'hyper-', and 'extra-' spaces we inhabit, or at least some of their aspects.

Restaurant in Seefeld, Tirol, Austria, 2023

A conjunction of different traditions by means of architecture, mixing the commodified images of alpine architecture and Chinese characters into a whole.

Today's space is seamlessly built upon juxtapositions and dislocations: conflicts between identities and new fluidities add to the rethinking of predefined categories, uses and imageries

Designing Conjunctions

But the question of how to give this space some form and significance persists. Architecture needs to understand the world by recognising that every space and form has multiple meanings, requirements, interpretations, uses and functions. To define a measure and a link between various times, traditions, expectations, identities, scales and demands is the challenge of creating new meanings for the many forms and practices that constitute the present space-time. As new customs, technologies and traditions alter physical environments and the way we experience them, it is imperative for architecture and design to provide expression to such becoming. In order to make sense of the forms that contemporary life takes in space, it is necessary to define plausible conjunctions. Even if we can no longer be utopians or nostalgic, we may still strive to strike a balance between our own wants and the collective good of a community, or whatever we want to call ourselves, while knowing that any plurality is not a homogeneous unicum. Perhaps it is still possible, in this sense, for architects and designers to *produce* meaning, and give form to likely realities.

When talking about 'sense' and 'meaning' in architecture and design we are referring to works that are grounded in the idea that they must once again face the world, its mundanity – both globally and locally – in terms of representation, praxis and recognition, while acknowledging the simultaneous variety and cohesion of the real. It is vital to learn to link the reality's multifaceted qualities, while being aware that, in today's world, 'science and art, reason and myth, are no longer contradictory poles, but give shape … to one homogeneous, indivisible discourse. It's a form of knowledge about life and its forms, which takes the same shape as the life it purports to apply to.'[10]

Conjunctions between the disjunctions of reality may turn architecture into a dialogical object capable of combining the many instances of the world. This should inevitably begin with a rejection of dissociations, naïve utopianism and onanistic subjectivism, in favour of combination, analysis and contemplation of the actual world within which one is operating. Only in this manner can architecture make sense of the world, reflect it, and give form to the contemporary needs to rediscover a plural dimension within the multiplicity of today's space and environment.

This is not to dismiss the value of anyone's own voice. It is self-evident that representation and analysis only exist in relation to expression and interpretation. After all, as poetically told by Borges, even the man who intended to sketch the whole world did nothing but draw 'a likeness of his own face'.[11] However, architectural design and theory may become practices establishing conjunctions between the parts of reality's manifold qualities. As demonstrated by the work of today's many architects, designers, historians, critics and artists, *our* practices and disciplines may be seen as needles stitching together material reality, the dreamt world, and socioeconomic relations, instead of producing mere innovation.

There is still a lot to see and do, especially in the near future, since what we normally refer to as modernisation is going through yet another self-inflicted crisis. For the time being, it might be useful to pick up everything that has been stated so far with a single line, while knowing that doing so carries the danger of creating a slogan.

There is a need for a refreshed attention to the real, for an interest in differences and paradoxes, in an attempt to construct plausible conjunctions between differences while envisioning spaces for today. ⌁

Giacomo Pala, Conjunction #2, 2023

Architectural composition: nature, geometry and objects as discrete elements, yet combined to make a conjunctive whole.

Giacomo Pala,
Conjunction #1,
2023

Architectural composition: a combination of forms, elements and nature, forging a combination of different conditions.

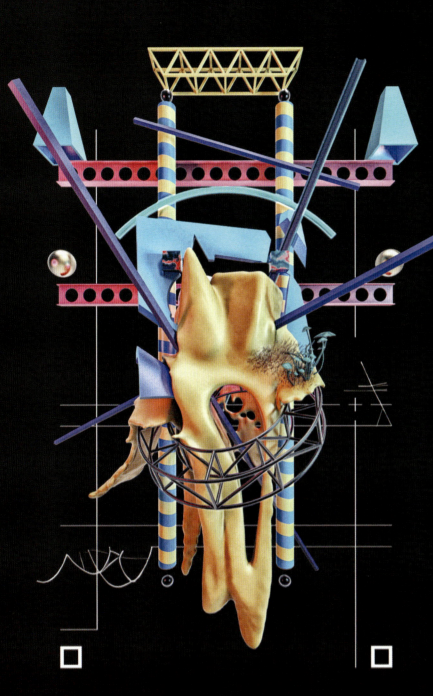

There is a need for a refreshed attention to the real, for an interest in differences and paradoxes, in an attempt to construct plausible conjunctions between differences while envisioning spaces for today

Notes
1. Rem Koolhaas, 'Junkspace' [2000], in Krista A Sykes and K Michael Hays (eds), *Constructing a New Agenda: Architectural Theory, 1993–2009*, Princeton Architectural Press (Princeton, NJ), 2010, p 137.
2. Bernard Tschumi, *Architecture and Disjunction*, MIT Press (Cambridge, MA), 1996, p 208.
3. Pier Vittorio Aureli, *The Possibility of an Absolute Architecture*, MIT Press (Cambridge, MA), 2011, p 205.
4. Hannah Arendt, *On Revolution*, Penguin Books (London), 6th edn, 1990, p 33.
5. Andrés Jaque, 'Grindr Archiurbanism', *Log* (No 41), 2017, p 77.
6. The Invisible Committee, *To Our Friends*, Semiotext(e) (London), 2015, p 188.
7. Gottfried Semper, 'The Four Elements of Architecture', in Harry Francis Mallgrave and Wolfgang Herrmann (eds), *The Four Elements of Architecture and Other Writings*, Cambridge University Press (Cambridge), 1989, p 102.
8. Carlo Rovelli, *Seven Brief Lessons on Physics*, Penguin Books (London), 2016, p 38. Kindle edition.
9. Timothy Morton, *Hyperobjects, Philosophy and Ecology after the End of the World*, University of Minnesota Press (Minneapolis, MN), 2013, p 116.
10. Emanuele Coccia, *Goods, Advertising, Urban Space, and the Moral Law of the Image*, Fordham University Press (New York), 2018, p 4.
11. Jorge Luis Borges, *The Aleph and Other Stories, 1933–1969*, Bantam Books (Toronto, New York and London), 1971, p 180.

Text © 2023 John Wiley & Sons Ltd.
Images © Giacomo Pala

Owen Hopkins

CELEB
THE

Ibiye Camp,
Still from *Market Stalls*
(film no 1),
2022

There has been street trading in Walworth, South London since the mid-16th century. East Street Market, which runs along East Street from Walworth Road to Dawes Street, has been running since 1880. The market traders and users reflect the area's amazing diversity, with stalls selling everything from clothing and cosmetics to fresh food. *Market Stalls* derives from a point-cloud study of the market, the dynamism of which resists other forms of architectural depiction.

RATING GLITCH

THE MULTISPATIAL WORK OF IBIYE CAMP

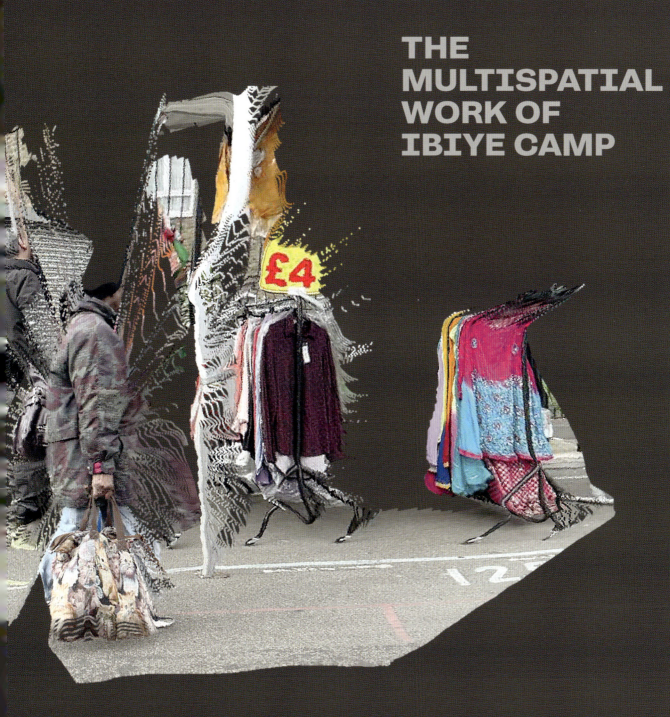

Artist Ibiye Camp exploits the supposed exactitude of digital technologies and uses its potential for glitches as imaginative tools. Her work focuses on the African continent and its diaspora. Guest-Editor **Owen Hopkins** talked to her about her working methods and the spatial opportunities they provide.

Architecture isn't neutral. All buildings, however mundane, are expressions of power, of their builders' ability to marshal the resources necessary to erect them. But not all buildings are architecture. One definition of architecture might be the art of making buildings that reflect not just their owners' ambitions, but meanings that are shared and held collectively. In other words, to transcend the (most often) private interests and perspectives of buildings' creators and speak to or even manifest public values and identities.

But while architecture frequently aspires to the status of a public art – and in effect a kind of equality of experience – the tools the discipline uses to depict, envision and, ultimately, to design are, like the resulting products, far from impartial. From the invention of single-point perspective, the plan, section and elevation, to the advent of photography and today's 3D modelling, architecture's tools reflect, and through that process serve to further embed, deeply entrenched hierarchies and value systems. The question, which takes us to the core of architecture's continuing relevance, is how it might find a way out of the resulting epistemological straightjacket.

For artist and educator Ibiye Camp, the answer lies in the messy intersections of the physical and digital that she explores through her multi-material, multidimensional and multidisciplinary practice.

Formative for Camp was the experience of East Street Market near where she grew up in Walworth, South London, 'a place that is very concentrated, where you have Indian shopkeepers selling Nigerian cuisine or sellers from Iraq selling vegetables grown in Croatia. These little ecosystems of trade and community made me quite interested in how we create.'

Coming initially from the perspective of art practice, Camp saw architecture – and in particular the Master's programme at the Royal College of Art – as a vehicle for thinking in new ways: 'I came into architecture not thinking that I would become a designer, but that it could be a way of articulating my artistic practice and help me think about the production of material and space.'

But the ways that architecture's tools of analysis act to determine how we see and understand those spaces soon became apparent: 'Representing people in architectural drawings – I found this very difficult. I was creating projects based in Lagos, in Balogun Market, and I very much struggled with the ideal imposed by the axonometric, for instance, which I felt flattened the various details of the building and how people would interact with the space.'

Multiple Ideals

Digital technology, and especially photogrammetry, offered a way to relieve this flattening, to move from two to three or more dimensions, and start a broader process of questioning the tensions inherent within what Camp calls 'the architectural language'. 'I'm very interested in creating a different type of language, a language of displacement or of different kinds of world views. Working with 3D scanning means working in a digital space where there are multiple ideals transposed from the physical world. There's a particular type of aesthetic in game space that's pristine or about creating a kind of a totality. I'm interested in when that breaks down: when there are conflicts, when digital forms collide with one another, when the rules of physics of the real world are bent. I'm fascinated by game spaces where you can fly.'

Photogrammetry has its own limitations, of course, and digital tools impose their own ways of working, processes and protocols that need to be followed. 'Photogrammetry has a lot of restrictions when it comes to certain types of material that you want to 3D scan,' says Camp. 'In my work I'm fascinated by scans that produce areas that are voided or where there are conflicts you have to navigate or move around.'

These voids and conflicts are partly a consequence of how photogrammetry works and the physics that underlies it. Yet they also betray the ideologies that permeate to a greater or lesser extent all digital technology: 'The software is designed for a still life or a very beautifully lit building, where the light re-bounces in a particular way. But if you want to use photogrammetry in a space that is super busy, densely populated with people and moving vehicles and things like that, even moving trees and the winds, that creates all sorts of errors and conflicts.'

However, for Camp these errors and conflicts are not absences or deficiencies in the data, but opportunities: 'I'm very interested in what is revealed through that error. The error might resemble a presence of someone or might resemble a kind of gap in the data pool of information.' In this sense, a void is place of potential, and while 'there's a power to not being able to be read or to be seen', as Camp admits, 'embracing or even celebrating the glitch', as she sees it, offers ways to foreground the overlooked or the marginalised – 'to re-imagine a space, to forge new alliances and new ways of seeing'.

Ibiye Camp,
Lapa Street,
Freetown,
Sierra Leone – still from
Data: the New Black Gold,
2019

opposite: *Data: the New Black Gold* explores how citizens could take ownership of the data generated from their cities to prevent exploitation. On site visits to Lagos, Nigeria and Freetown, Sierra Leone, documentation was made of the most populated streets and markets of the city. A series of informal mobile devices called Area Snap allowed a digital city to be collected, formed, stored, multiplied, valued and ultimately owned by its citizens.

Ibiye Camp,
Mangos on Campbell Street,
Freetown,
Sierra Leone – still from
Data: the New Black Gold,
2019

left: Using photogrammetry, which opposes Western architectural ideals of modelling, Area Snap made scans at multiple viewpoints: ground view, eye view and bird's-eye view. The resulting film shows the imperfect city and explores the bias and conflicts of digital and technological infrastructures in West Africa.

Ibiye Camp,
Remaining Threads,
3D-printed model of
Kalabari Ceremony,
13th Shanghai Biennale,
2021

The ever-changing Injiri cloth production is rendered in 3D models and sculptures of distorted scenes, which become ghosts of what once populated the manufacturing process, their incompleteness pointing to the possibility of alternative pasts/futures. Surrounded by the beats of Kalabari drums, sound, object and film combine to create a multispace of resistance.

Ibiye Camp,
Still from *Remaining Threads* (no 2),
13th Shanghai Biennale,
2021

Remaining Threads utilises 3D-scanning technologies to explore the transformation of textile production in Buguma, Nigeria. Kalabari craftwomen had historically reimagined Madras cloth by cutting and removing threads to create Injiri cloth, which is worn in Kalabari ceremonies. In recent years, machines have been introduced in the production of Injiri, supplanting traditional practices and marking a shift in social roles, technologies, aesthetics and institutions.

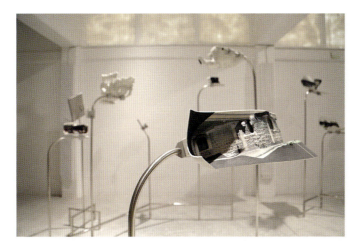

Ibiye Camp,
Sacred Forest of Ethiopia,
Sharjah Architecture Triennial,
UAE,
2019

Presented at the 2019 Sharjah Architecture Triennial in collaboration with Emmy Bacharach and David Killingsworth, *Sacred Forests of Ethiopia* uses photogrammetry to document the sacred spaces of forest and church at ground level. In contrast to the completeness of aerial imagery, the documentation and resultant exhibition installation is unresolved, conjuring a place of multiplicity and potential.

New Languages

Even today, the default mode for an architect looking to analyse a site is via a sketch in-situ, with all its attendant subjectivities and biases embedded in the conventions of architectural depiction. A scan, in contrast, at least in the hands of Camp, is more like a transcript – one that, in this guise, serves to 'intensify dialogues that are missing from normative perceptions of public space'. Camp's practice is, therefore, not simply concerned with the new possibilities that digital tools afford, but just like her approach to architecture, about 'interrogating' them.

Part of this interrogation focuses on the way digital technology reflects ideals and ideologies that are decidedly Western. Most technology still emanates physically and ideologically from the West – indeed, from a small part of California – while the data sets that are increasingly central to its development are concentrated in both actual Western places and in broader Western notions of space.

Alongside her practice and teaching in London, Camp spends part of the year in Sierra Leone, from which context the extent that architecture and its technological apparatus 'has been developed with these ideals which are still are very Western' is readily apparent. Thus, supplementing these Western architectural languages with 'new languages that can come from the Global South and reflect its traditional practices of space' is an enduring concern.

These 'new languages' foregrounded by Camp in her work pose challenges to the ways architecture is designed, but also the cultures in which that takes place. With very few exceptions, architects still operate in studio-based silos where knowledge and expertise is proprietary. Although Camp herself is not a coder, she sees herself as part of 'a huge community of coders in Unity [the real-time game development platform] that share knowledge, making freely all manner of add-ons, packages and assets that you can include in your work'.

Thinking about Camp's early and recurring interest in the cultures of markets, it is no surprise she is drawn to this 'shared community where everyone's sharing skills'. For architecture itself, as her work makes so vividly clear, there is much to learn not only from the new possibilities and perspectives offered by the digital world, but, to use Camp's words, from the 'space almost of public knowledge' that has grown up around it. ᴆ

All quotes in this article are from a video-call interview with the author on 30 January 2023.

Text © 2023 John Wiley & Sons Ltd.
Images © Ibiye Camp

Joshua Bard and Francesca Torello

ARCHITECTURE IS INTERFACE

LATENT VIRTUALITY FROM ANTIQUITY TO ZOOM

Xin Chen, Min-Young Jeong
and Denise Jiang,
Soane House - Our House,
'Low-Relief' Advanced Synthesis
Option Studio,
Carnegie Mellon University,
Pittsburgh, Pennsylvania,
2020

In response to pandemic isolation, the project explored the spatial continuum of the students' physical rooms, the digital spaces of their daily collaboration, and the additional spatial presence of their collections and models of architecture, both physical and digital. This student team's design highlights a heightened awareness of private and public spaces where the computer camera's cone of vision demarcates this hybrid reality.

Architectural educators **Joshua Bard and Francesca Torello** embrace numerous digital technologies to subvert issues of scale, framing, materiality, inside and outside to provoke viewers into contemplating the current nature of architecture and its discourse. Their inspiration is Sir John Soane's Museum in London, which is a multilayered conversation between objects and their interrelationships with themselves and their settings.

... the virtual, strictly defined, has little relationship to that which is false, illusory, or imaginary. The virtual is by no means the opposite of the real. On the contrary, it is a fecund and powerful mode of being that expands the process of creation, opens up the future, injects a core of meaning beneath the platitude of immediate physical presence.
— Pierre Lévy, Becoming Virtual: Reality in the Digital Age, 1998[1]

In March of 2020, at the onset of the Covid-19 pandemic, we found ourselves scrambling to adjust our jointly taught architecture studio at Carnegie Mellon University to remote teaching. Like other educators around the globe we quickly cobbled together a multi-platform, online infrastructure to facilitate remote learning. What was different for us, however, was our studio's focus on architecture and virtual reality.

For the past six years we have been collaboratively working and teaching at the intersection of our shared interests: as an architectural historian exploring buildings' mediatic power and as a design educator focused on the historical roots of contemporary technology. While virtual reality (VR) and augmented reality (AR) technologies are often pitched against bricks-and-mortar architecture or described as 'a possible distraction from the real world',[2] a sophisticated culture of hybrid, physical and virtual spaces consistently runs through architecture's history, well before the digital. Hybrid spaces are actually a core strength of architecture's disciplinary past.

The contention that because of this past history architects have something meaningful to contribute when it comes to contemporary AR technologies became an active experiment in response to the studio's remote modality. Conducting an architecture studio via Zoom quickly transitioned from a logistical challenge to a spatial exploration. The final assignment was reframed to respond to our new life conditions: the demarcations between public and private space were being carefully renegotiated through our cameras' cones of view and virtual backgrounds, while our screens provided both the essential connection of our worlds to each other and an escape route to other realities. It seemed obvious to explore that continuum, those portals and wormholes, the interconnected physical-visual-virtual spaces we were all floating in.

Sir John Soane's house/office/museum, with its illusionistic, multimedia apparatuses, offered the starting point for reimagining the de facto multispace confronting us. In the project 'Soane House – Our House' (undertaken within the 'Low Relief' Advanced Synthesis Option Studio at Carnegie Mellon University in 2020), the disparate physical and digital dimensions of the students' collaborative work were explored as composite architectural spaces, showing the students' forthright adjustment to designing with the connections and spill-outs between physical and virtual.

The forced modalities of life in a pandemic allowed us to more clearly recognise a hybridisation process, which from well before the emergency we had anticipated as a relevant and consequential site of architectural research.

Sir John Soane,
The Dome Area,
Sir John Soane's Museum,
London,
1837

Sir John Soane's Museum provides a prototypical analogue multispace, where architecture, media, and artefacts create a complex, multilayered experience.

Interfaces: Mediating Human Experience
Architecture can be described as an interface, mediating the hybrid strata of reality – physical to virtual, imagined and real. Buildings are many-layered, complex entities that at times create portals to illusionistic spaces, transporting us and expanding our awareness beyond the empirical scope of everyday life. Like other interfaces, architecture operates in the background, shaping the underlying structures for human activity.

The 'latent virtuality' of pre-digital architecture was obtained with precise shaping of physical materials across multiple media, resulting in complex spatial relationships and combining towards synthetic experiential ends. Decorative motifs seamlessly transitioned from columns to mouldings, from sculptures to frescos, spanning multiple dimensions of human perception, from 3D (architectural elements) to 2.5D (low-relief sculpture), 2D (flat surface treatments) and, where direct sunlight was present, time.

This savoir-faire, traditions and practices – and at times even crafts and materials – were suppressed from the discipline of architecture under the weight of the Modernist dogma against illusion and in favour of a certain kind of authenticity. They are only recently being rediscovered, in part because of their role in anticipating some of the workings of contemporary technologies, as illustrated by the following discussion of three techniques of virtualisation in architecture.

Buildings are many-layered, complex entities that at times create portals to illusionistic spaces, transporting us and expanding our awareness beyond the empirical scope of everyday life. Like other interfaces, architecture operates in the background, shaping the underlying structures for human activity

Framing: Organising Layers of Reality

Frames, one of the building blocks of architecture, demarcate transitions between spaces, create focal points for our attention, and organise our visual field.[3] Frames condition lived experience, but can also encourage a probing of the boundaries of the real and the possible. Careful calibration between frame and content can create depth where there is none, or flatten spaces receding in the distance. The multiplicity and interlocking of frames provides a rich perceptual field, where from a single vantage point observers can experience at once near and far, real and imagined spaces.

In our own work environment, the early 20th-century Pittsburgh campus of the Carnegie Institute of Technology, today Carnegie Mellon University, compelling examples of framing enhance the sheer theatricality of the design of landscape, exterior and interior spaces of the Beaux-Arts campus. The apparently conventional masterplan, with its academic buildings clustered around open lawns, actually required a complicated application of sectional design and the use of trompe l'oeil to circumvent the difficult topography of Pittsburgh. Highly visible framing devices help create a visual tension between the centres of art and industry, placed as focal points at the far edges of the campus in sustained conversation with each other.[4]

The same main axis continues inside the College of Fine Arts building, traversing the multiple interlocking frames of the entry sequence within its Great Hall – completed to Henry Hornbostel's designs in 1915 – and focusing the visitor's gaze on the office of the Dean, where the monumental plaster cast of a Baroque entrance portal is deceivingly used as an interior door frame.

The student installation *Magic Box* (2019) activated these design elements of the Great Hall by carefully inserting a frame that uses projection mapping of drone footage and anamorphic projection to unlock the sequential spatial logic of the campus's primary axis from a single vantage point.

Henry Hornbostel,
Great Hall,
College of Fine Arts,
Carnegie Mellon University,
Pittsburgh, Pennsylvania,
1915

The Great Hall's entry sequence deploys interlocking frames to emphasise the positioning of the building's main entrance on the organising axis of the campus plan, then drives the eye to the plaster cast portal framing the entrance to the Dean's office, placed a few steps above the main space of the Hall and at the visitor's eye level.

Keon Ho Lee, Michael Powell
and Dingkun Wang,
Magic Box, in the Great Hall,
'Low-Relief' Advanced
Synthesis Option Studio,
Carnegie Mellon University,
Pittsburgh, Pennsylvania,
2019

Students explored aerial surveillance, anamorphic projection and projection mapping in conversation with similar techniques used at the turn of the 20th century by the building's architect, Henry Hornbostel. Drone footage captured along the campus's primary axis was projected onto a plaster model in the Great Hall, further accentuating Hornbostel's deliberate blurring of interior and exterior spaces throughout the campus design.

Henry Hornbostel,
Great Hall,
College of Fine Arts,
Carnegie Mellon University,
Pittsburgh, Pennsylvania,
1915

above: A substitute to educational travel experiences and inspired by the architect's own European tour, the ceiling painting by James Monroe Hewlett includes an extensive collection of architectural references. The larger images seem to carry the visitor away to lively locales, while smaller vignettes of other buildings of importance and architectural details and fragments dotted along the ornamental bands add to the pedagogical value, which at the time was based on the repetition of the canon.

Francesca Torello and Joshua Bard,
Virtual Fresco mixed-reality app,
College of Fine Arts,
Carnegie Mellon University,
Pittsburgh, Pennsylvania,
2022

below: Conceived to help visitors of the College of Fine Arts explore the painted vault of the Great Hall through augmented reality, the project is based on the premise that the ceiling itself was already designed to transport the viewer to faraway sites and buildings – just not yet with digital tools.

Perspective: the Spatial Scaffold of Perception
The design of the Great Hall reveals other exciting lessons, this time about projection and its ability to organise the built environment – a second technique that pervades the history of the discipline[5] and which, because of its synthetic capacity, is also a key driver of architecture's relationship to the virtual.

Image capture and projection help conjure up an immaterial geometric scaffold, which can be generative for the design of buildings or work as a mechanism for shaping our perceptual experience in the built environment. The fundamental components of perspective – such as projection lines, vantage points and view cones – encourage our creative capacity to extend to imagined space the shapes and spatial relationships that architecture is only partially hinting at in physical form.

The large mural on the Great Hall's vaulted ceiling, which was added shortly after the building's construction, is an elegantly arranged collection of precedents from architecture and sculpture, mapped to the features of the vault and interspersed with references to music, painting and the literary arts. The architectural scenes were created by projecting and tracing lantern slides, the same ones available in the Carnegie Tech teaching collection.[6] In a reverse visual effect, the content of the mural, floating high above, seems to stream back to the viewer's eyes at ground level. From a central location on the floor of the hall, viewers are enveloped in a refracted array of images closely aligned with their vantage point.

The Great Hall was designed to function as a (pre-digital) immersive pedagogical experience. In our AR project Virtual Fresco (2022), the many educational features of the space, designed to work in the mind of an early 20th-century architecture student, were used to create a digital media experience that reproduces and clarifies their functioning for a contemporary visitor. Virtual Fresco allows at the same time an enriched, immersive experience of the space, a deeper appreciation for its layered design and a clear understanding of its proto-virtual capabilities.

Gallery display,
east wall,
Hall of Architecture,
Carnegie Museum of Art,
Pittsburgh, Pennsylvania,
1907

A number of monumental, standalone pieces, a selection from the more than 150 fragments in this collection, illustrate how the uniformity of plaster allows comparison of architectural elements that vary in style, era and geographic origin, while at the same time each piece faithfully represents the different materiality of the original – smooth marble, rough and ageing stone, and even wood and bronze.

Materiality: the Hyper Reality of Faux Finishes
Buildings are materially intensive, and this constraint is often pitted against the rising tide of virtualisation.[7] The assumption is that physical buildings are 'real' and virtual environments are 'fake'. Yet a historical framing of 'faux', pre-digital materials in architecture uncovers a number of parallels that complicate this seemingly antagonistic binary.

Plaster is an especially fitting example of a 'real' material that in the characteristics and possibilities of its seemingly 'faux' applications works as a pre-digital, analogue counterpart of the surface treatments we see applied in digital space. Plaster is the ideal faux material; it is a highly plastic, monochromatic substrate, applied seamlessly across architectural elements – from wall to moulding to ceiling; it can also be finished with hyper specificity of surface texture and colour. The combination of these traits is an embodied contradiction. Plaster is a non-material, yet it can become every material. The 'fakeness' of plaster is not the absence of concrete materiality, but instead the oversaturation of a too-perfect realness.

At the turn of the 20th century, plaster was an ideal material to obtain high-fidelity replicas, an important vehicle of mass-instruction in an era of still relatively expensive and hard-to-find photographs and limited travel opportunities. It was common for schools to have collections of smaller fragments for pedagogical purposes,[8] while museums housed large and monumental plaster cast collections.[9] One of the few cast collections of architecture that still survive today is the Hall of Architecture at the Carnegie Museum of Art in Pittsburgh (1907).

In the museum's gallery, forms from disparate geographic regions and time periods are made orderly and comparable by being uniformly cast in plaster, yet the same material also adapts to show different surface treatments and levels of ageing, connecting each replica in the museum with its original elsewhere in the world. The hyper-real materiality and three-dimensionality of the plaster pieces were necessary cues that the viewer needed to be able to conjure up the original building, just as credible material effects give substance to the immersive environments that we traverse and experience in the digital realm today.

In fact, the Hall provides a 'virtual tour' within its walls. In this regard, historical collections of plaster casts of architecture are a precedent of contemporary virtual reality. Just like AR experiences, they collapse space and time, encouraging unexpected juxtapositions and the ability to curate and organise fragments to form new structures of understanding.

Our AR project Plaster ReCast (2018) was designed to make the layered, complex workings of this collection legible to contemporary visitors by using digital media.[10] The fragments in the museum are also aliases, which represent the entry point into the larger, virtual and three-dimensional space that the visitor can explore and learn about.

Synthetic Spaces

The techniques of virtualisation in architecture are rarely found in isolation and are more often deployed in combination, to heightened effect. The techniques, precedent and projects discussed in this article illustrate how architecture has long probed multiple dimensions of reality and serves as a connecting bridge between physical and virtual experience.

To uncover architecture's latent virtuality suggests a continuation of concern and technique in architectural design that is ideally situated to inform contemporary practice and its relation with technology. Framing architecture as a reality interface foregrounds the task ahead: as immersive technologies become more interactive, and the built environment more adaptive, designers have a real opportunity to shape the synthetic spaces of the future. ⌾

Notes
1. Pierre Lévy, *Becoming Virtual: Reality in the Digital Age*, Plenum Trade (New York), 1998, p 16.
2. Pamela Buxton, 'Opportunities: The Metaverse', *The RIBA Journal*, 12 April 2022: https://www.ribaj.com/intelligence/the-metaverse-a-virtual-opportunity-or-a-distraction-from-real-world-work.
3. See Bernard Cache, *Earth Moves: The Furnishing of Territories*, MIT Press (Cambridge, MA), 1998.
4. See Martin Aurand, *The Spectator and the Topographical City*, University of Pittsburgh Press (Pittsburgh, PA), 2006, pp 136–201.
5. See Robin Evans, *The Projective Cast: Architecture and its Three Geometries*, MIT Press (Cambridge, MA), 1995.
6. See Charles Rosenblum, *The Architecture of Henry Hornbostel: Progressive and Traditional Design in the American Beaux-Arts Movement*, PhD thesis, University of Virginia, 2009. On the Great Hall's pedagogical function, see Francesca Torello, 'History to Look At: Mediating Architectural History in Turn of the Twentieth Century Pittsburgh', in Salvador Guerrero and Joaquín Medina Warmburg (eds), *Lo Construido y lo Pensado – Built and Thought: European and Transatlantic Correspondences in the Historiography of Architecture*, Asociación de Historiadores de la Arquitectura y el Urbanismo (Madrid), 2022, pp 566–80.
7. See Antoine Picon, *The Materiality of Architecture*, University of Minnesota Press (Minneapolis, MN), 2020.
8. See Mark Wigley, 'Prosthetic Theory: The Disciplining of Architecture', *Assemblage*, 15, August 1991, pp 7–29, and Katherine Wheeler, 'A Tangible Past: Casts in British Architectural Education', *ARRIS: The Journal of the Southeast Chapter of the Society of Architectural Historians*, 23, 2012, pp 2–15.
9. See Mari Lending, *Plaster Monuments: Architecture and the Power of Reproduction*, Princeton University Press (Princeton, NJ), 2017.
10. The app was developed by the authors in collaboration with the Carnegie Mellon Entertainment Center and Carnegie Museum of Art: see https://vimeo.com/246512552.

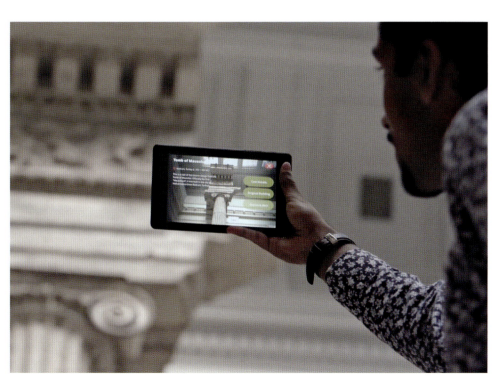

Francesca Torello and Joshua Bard with the Carnegie Mellon University Entertainment Technology Center and Carnegie Museum of Art, Plaster ReCast mixed-reality app, Pittsburgh, Pennsylvania, 2018

Plaster ReCast is based on the interplay between the virtual and physical dimensions of cast collections – the required mental effort of imagining the original building, which cannot be present in the gallery space; its didactic connections to history, geography and archaeology; and the physical experience of observing highly crafted artefacts in spatial juxtaposition to each other.

Text © 2023 John Wiley & Sons Ltd. Images: pp 78–9 © Xin Chen, Min-Young Jeong, Denise Jiang; p 81 Photo courtesy Owen Hopkins; p 82(t) photograph by Pablo Garcia, used with permission; pp 82(b) © Keon Ho Lee, Michael Powell, Dingkun Wang; p 83(t) Photo Dllu, Attribution-ShareAlike 4.0 International (CC BY-SA 4.0): https://creativecommons.org/licenses/by-sa/4.0/deed.en; pp 83(b), 85 © Joshua Bard and Francesca Torello; p 84 © Luc Merx

RY ART
and Multispace

Andrew Kovacs

Very Big Art uses a variety of both virtual and real media to create a nexus where architecture, the public realm, urban design, performance, ephemerality and art meet at an often colossal scale – a 21st-century reworking of the notion of the architectural 'folly'. Architectural designer and educator **Andrew Kovacs** describes a brief history of some of the early exponents of arch-art, and leads us through some recent examples, including the output of his own practice.

Architecture is a public art because it is by nature public.
— James Wines, *De-Architecture*, 1987[1]

Architectural follies became prevalent during the 18th century as common features of landscape gardens across Europe, though most notably in England. Often highly ornate, formally adventurous and idiosyncratic in conception, follies as a type are defined by their lack of practical function. They were typically conceived as ornamental rather than practical, used to explore new or emerging architectural styles or ideas, as eyecatchers in the landscape, or as places to meet or entertain.

Follies continued to be built well into the 19th century, however they all but disappeared in the 20th. Now, in the 21st century, they are making a comeback. One of the most notable – or notorious – of recent years is *Vessel* by Thomas Heatherwick at Hudson Yards in New York, which opened in 2019. It stands alongside another structure that strictly speaking is not a folly, but which manifests many of the same characteristics: Diller Scofidio + Renfro's The Shed, an arts and cultural centre that opened the same year.

The Kebab and the Handbag

The structures' (self-consciously) unusual forms – and the even more unusual combination they make – has attracted widespread comment, most damningly from Oliver Wainwright, the architecture critic of *The Guardian*, who in a Tweet described the two structures as the Kebab and the Handbag, complete with mocking photo. Notwithstanding these criticisms, it is instructive to analyse their formation and role as follies in more detail.

The Shed is an archetype of contemporary high architecture, a novel, quasi-public building marked by the way large components can physically move in order, in the architects' words, 'to support artists' most ambitious ideas'.[2] Reflecting the institutions' desire to reach 'all audiences', The Shed is a space where any imaginable setting for art might occur as a result of the architecture literally moving to accommodate art (in contrast to the more usual example of art having to adapt to the architecture of where it is displayed).

Vessel by Heatherwick Studio and
The Shed by Diller Scofidio + Renfro,
New York City,
2019

pages 86–87: The Shed and *Vessel*, along with the High Line park, form a network dedicated to leisure and fun. This contemporary public space is different to public spaces of the past, partly through its designers' attempt to crossover concepts from art and architecture.

James Gibbs,
Temple of Liberty,
Stowe, Buckinghamshire,
UK,
1741

right: One of the most important examples of the English landscape garden, the garden at Stowe is littered with a huge range of temples, archways and statues drawing from the classical tradition. In contrast, James Gibbs's Temple of Liberty is an early example of the Gothic revival, with the style deployed – as would become typical in the early 19th century – to invoke the apparent medieval origins of English liberty.

Vessel takes this idea further, with the architecture itself becoming the work of art. As a structure, *Vessel* is at a scale and has the permanence to constitute architecture. However, it is architecture comprising just stairs and structure – an architecture with no roof, no façade and no windows. As its designers' website explains, their mission was 'To create something meaningful, … a structure that visitors could use, touch and relate to … a new landmark that could be climbed and explored.'[3]

In conception and practice, The Shed and *Vessel* have much in common: both draw from ideas and approaches from art as well as architecture, both structures are people attractors, both produce spatial-cultural experiences, and both aim to engage audiences in a heightened way. Situated next to one another, and adjacent to the top of the High Line – a disused elevated railway repurposed as a park, which is itself another kind of folly – The Shed and *Vessel* help fashion a contemporary collective space dedicated to leisure. Together, the two structures demonstrate the phenomenon of Very Big Art.

Multispatial Architecture

When art is too big to be inside a museum, it necessarily enters the territory of architecture and public. When art becomes as big as a building, it takes on certain aspects of architecture while leaving others behind. When art, architecture, urbanism, landscape and public space collide, they do so in the realm of Very Big Art, which offers possibilities for new forms of collectivity that reflect the increasingly physical/digital hybridised world in which we live.

Very Big Art differs considerably from earlier forms of public art. To take one canonical example, at the Kluczynski Federal Building in Chicago (1974), the distinction between art and architecture is clear. Alexander Calder's expressive figurative sculpture *Flamingo* (1974) is surrounded by the pristine geometric architectural masses of Mies van der Rohe.

The relationship between art and architecture is spatially straightforward – there is the architecture and then there is the art. Yet often such highly formal relationships result in spaces that may be public in theory but are not public in practice, bringing to mind the cliché of the windswept Modernist plaza.

This relationship between art, architecture and public space with Very Big Art is more open, flexible, ambiguous and potentially more collective. As in the examples of The Shed and *Vessel*, Very Big Art has more in common with the experience of exploring an outdoor museum or a shopping mall in search of spaces to hang out, have a meal, take a selfie or simply enjoy a stroll.

Wainwright is far from the only critic to take aim at *Vessel*, which is frequently seen in the context of its role in the Hudson Yards mega-development as emblematic of the corporatisation of New York City (and of cities more broadly). Yet among the public it has been a huge success, becoming a destination – like the High Line before it – even if it is functionless in the conventional sense.

To understand this divergence in response, a clue might be found in the fact that much of the criticism levelled at *Vessel* has emanated from social media. This is both fitting and ironic because in many ways the structure was created with those platforms in mind. Even if its designers and commissioners would not admit to it, it was quite clearly conceived to create experiences that are celebrated and amplified as shareable on social media.

Operating as both a backdrop and a space for these excursions, marking a place, a moment in time and creating a destination, *Vessel* exists in the city and on social media. In this way, Very Big Art is a hybrid not just in its status as both art and architecture, but in the way it operates in the physical *and* digital worlds. Whether consciously or not, Very Big Art is architecture created specifically for the new condition of multispace.

Alexander Calder,
Flamingo,
Kluczynski Federal Building,
Chicago, Illinois,
1974

The *Flamingo* and the Miesian boxes of the Kluczynski Federal Building demonstrate the old, Modernist distinction between public space, public art and architecture. The scale of the public art is visibly smaller than the architecture surrounding it, dwarfing it in a large open public plaza.

Arch-Art in the 21st century
In his 1987 book *De-Architecture*, the artist-architect James Wines wrote: 'Recent environmental artists have ... developed a range of totemic applications of architecture that, for lack of a better term, might be called "arch-art." This hybrid form has produced sculptures and land pieces that incorporate methodology and iconography of buildings.'[4] Very Big Art is an evolution of Arch-Art – public art scaled up that productively bumps into other disciplines, such as urban design and landscape design, to produce collective spaces.

However, with regard to the positive impacts of the new tendency Wines identified and described, he was more equivocal: 'In terms of environmental art's potential lessons for public art and architecture, this attitude has led to a crisis of missed opportunities.'[5]

Fast-forward to our present and it is clear how Arch-Art has pervasively influenced contemporary culture. These missed opportunities that Wines lamented have inverted to seemingly endless opportunities. From art parks to festivals, pop-up installations, temporary and permanent pavilions, follies, design-build workshops, public performances, plop art and public art, Arch-Art is everywhere. Very Big Art increases not just its size, but its spectacle, audience, interactivity and frequency. Very Big Art brings together and exists through multiple scales and temporalities.

While *Vessel* points to a new paradigm for public space, its critics are right in taking aim at the corporate ideologies that underpin it and which it helps enable, as well as the ways access and behaviour are controlled and the formal limitations of the structure itself. New progressive models are needed to realise the transformative potential of Very Big Art in allowing for different and competing ideas, narratives and power structures to coexist and interact both in the physical world and in the digital one – models that the work of Office Kovacs is exploring and developing.

Office Kovacs,
Supertall Superobject,
'Model Behavior' exhibition,
The Cooper Union,
New York City,
2022

above right: Supertall Superobject is a model for a conceptual proposal for collective living, suggesting an alternative approach to the New York super-tall towers. It takes the form of a vertical conglomerate composed of objects that rise to the height of a skyscraper.

right: As a model, Supertall Superobject is made through hybridising traditional architectural model-making techniques with physical 3D collage. It is composed of ready-made, recognisable parts that have been altered through physical model-making and combined to form a new whole.

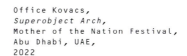

Office Kovacs,
Superobject Arch,
Mother of the Nation Festival,
Abu Dhabi, UAE,
2022

left: A superobject is a collection of recognisable objects that are contiguous. As such, this contiguous collection arches to form a folly. The photo is an iPhone capture printed on an instax printer and then digitised on a flatbed scanner.

below left: Superobject Arch was a pop-up portal along the main pedestrian path at the Mother of the Nation Festival. The project was conceived through a series of digital collages. The content for these collages was found objects digitised on a flatbed scanner that were collected through the office's Archive of Affinities project.

Progressive Models

If art allows people to perceive and visualise the world in new ways, and if architecture allows people to inhabit and occupy the world in new ways, then Very Big Art is a hybrid territory of practice where new structures devoted to collective and common spaces can be produced. The ongoing image-collection project Archive of Affinities collects examples of these follies, arch-art and architectural B-sides, and the practice Office Kovacs produces them.

The physical models produced for exhibitions offer speculations towards the quest for Very Big Art. Drawing from the Archive of Affinities, the content of these models consists of collected and altered found objects, constructed through a freestyle model-making manner that hybridises traditional architecture techniques with physical 3D collage. As such, the physical models, through their configuration, composition and contiguity, suggest a new totality of inhabitable worlds.

While these models remain speculative, in parallel Office Kovacs has produced public installations for numerous festivals which can be understood as further experiments towards Very Big Art. Created for the Mother of the Nation Festival in Abu Dhabi, UAE, in 2022, *Superobject Arch* is a composition, arranged seemingly at random, of six recognisable objects at different relative scales. A lemon, a house, a building, a full popcorn container, a balloon and a box stack twist and connect to form a 'superobject' that arches over the pedestrian path. The composition was generated by content shared on the Archive of Affinities, specifically a scan that contains a collection of found objects from previous physical models. The parts of this scan were then digitally collaged in elevation, within the allotted dimensions, to form an archway over a public pathway.

Office Kovacs,
Colossal Cacti,
Coachella Valley Music
and Arts Festival,
Indio, California,
2019

Colossal Cacti was a series of stylised and overscaled Saguaro cacti to create a temporary quasi-public space at Coachella. The space was activated physically as a plaza and digitally through a significant quantity of images shared on social media platforms.

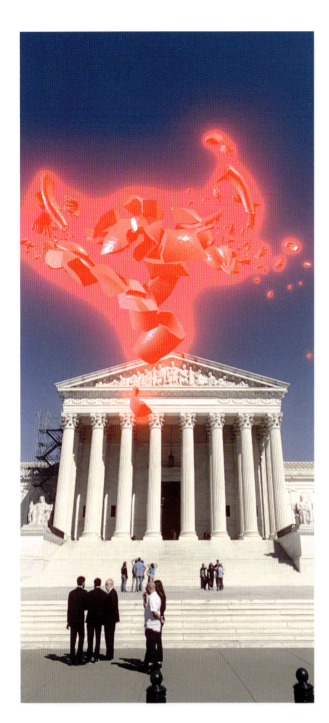

Nancy Baker Cahill,
State Property,
Supreme Court Building,
Washington DC,
2023,

Created as a response to the overturning of Roe versus Wade in 2022 and the subsequent curtailing of abortion rights in the US, Nancy Baker Cahill's *State Property* was 'installed' in augmented reality (AR) above the Supreme Court Building via the 4th Wall App. Comprising a bright-red uterus that breaks apart, the work and its provocative siting vividly illustrated the way the uterus has become a location of contestation and violence, while pointing to the potential for AR and of multispace more broadly to allow new forms of protest and public artistic expression.

Very Big Art opens not just new ways of making and doing architecture, but new forms of collectivity and of being together

In the era of the smartphone, the free and endless circulation of images on social media not only reconceptualises our idea of public space but also reinvigorates the role architecture may have in setting the stage to encourage the public to perform and act. An example of this is the Office Kovacs project *Colossal Cacti*, which consisted of seven large sculptural cacti loosely arranged in a spiralling ring formation to create a plaza and entryway for the 2019 Coachella Valley Music and Arts Festival in Indio, California. At the base of each of the seven cacti was a stepped plinth, inviting festival-goers to rest, dance on top, meet up, lounge in the shade, people-watch or listen to music. All seven cacti were covered in bright colours that up close provided a playful backdrop while from a distance made the overall configuration appear like a sprawling cacti skyline. Throughout the event, *Colossal Cacti* became one of the most photographed atmospheres, rendering the project iconic on the internet through a mosh pit of selfies.

The discipline of architecture has long produced utopian, heroic, imaginary, fantastical and critical works that visualise profound changes to everyday life. Very Big Art continues that tradition. But where in the past these ideas, with a few notable exceptions, were confined to the drawing board, the advent of multispace provides new avenues to realise them. Architecture now exists in two realms – the physical and the digital – and its impact is no longer dependent on its materiality but on the ideas it contains, the reactions they engender, the attentions they sustain and the behaviours they enable. Very Big Art opens not just new ways of making and doing architecture, but new forms of collectivity and of being together. ⌀

Notes
1. James Wines, *De-Architecture*, Rizzoli (New York), 1987, p 113.
2. See https://dsrny.com/project/the-shed.
3. See https://www.heatherwick.com/project/vessel/.
4. Wines, *op cit*, p 101.
5. *Ibid*, p 91.

Text © 2023 John Wiley & Sons Ltd. Images: pp 86–7 © François Roux/Shutterstock; p 88 © A C Manley/Shutterstock; p 89 © Roy Harris/Shutterstock; pp 90–91 © Office Kovacs; p 92 © Phil Donohue; p 93 © Nancy Baker Cahill

Keiken,
Player of Cosmic ༗´º Realms,
'WORLDBUILDING: Gaming
and Art in the Digital Age'
exhibition,
Julia Stoschek Collection,
Düsseldorf,
2022

Artist collective Keiken's work speculates on future entanglements of humanity and technology. *Player of Cosmic ༗´º Realms*, debuted in 2022, is an interactive installation that allows players to temporarily experience life with an artificial womb.

Alice Bucknell

WAYS OF WORLDING
BUILDING ALTERNATIVE FUTURES IN MULTISPACE

The integration of the real and the digital – particularly gaming engines – offers architects and designers the opportunity to develop narrative environments that can be predicated on speculative fiction. Such spaces, landscapes and buildings explore magical panoramas created not just by human ingenuity, but also by machine and nonhuman intelligence. Artist and writer Alice Bucknell takes us into some of these possible worlds.

Ian Cheng,
Life After BOB: The Chalice Study,
Halle am Berghain,
Berlin,
2021

below: Located within the sprawling concrete environment of Berghain, Berlin's most infamous nightclub, this multimedia installation considers the increasingly blurry boundary between humans and artificial intelligence.

below: Tapping into Cheng's 'world-watching station', viewers become active directors in the work's narrative.

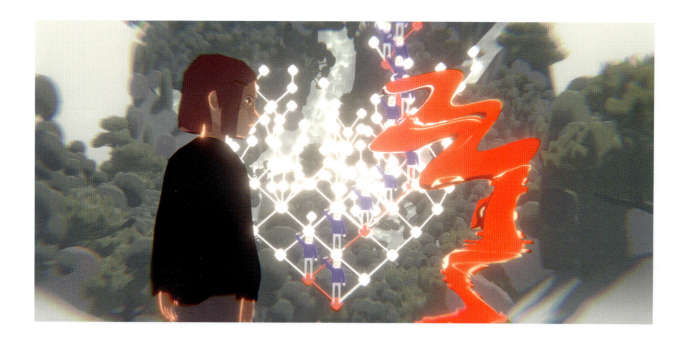

above: Stills from *Life After BOB*. Cheng creates novel forms of open-ended and mutable cinematic narratives generated with game-engine technology.

Sprawled out on a white futon in the Luma Foundation's neo-industrial Zurich outpost, phone in hand, I am invited into the 'worldwatching station' of simulation artist Ian Cheng's feature-length CGI film, *Life After BOB: The Chalice Study* (2021). Centred around a 10-year-old girl named Chalice Wong, whose brain has been fitted with an AI implant, the film explores the ever-evolving mediations of technology and the self. Using my phone as both a remote and console, I can explore Cheng's narrative world: pausing, rewinding, and homing in on the story's specific characters. As the film plays out in front of me, I wave my phone around in the direction of the screen, pulling up more information through a crowd-sourced 'BOBipedia': a collaborative database on the work that viewers can edit in real time, leaving behind lore for the next worldwatcher.

Cheng is best known for creating hypnotic and dizzying open-world simulations including the *Emissaries* trilogy (2015–18). These are AI-powered video game environments that play themselves, weird virtual landscapes bristling with an aliveness that teeters between past and future, imminent apocalypse and infinite duration. While Cheng's worlds began as autonomous agents, recent iterations like *Life After BOB* arc towards public intervention, reframing the white cube as something akin to a gamer's chair. This pivot from passive viewer to active player, a palpable transition within digital art ecosystems as well as adjacent fields of architecture and design in recent years, signifies a broader attitude shift in how gaming slots into visual culture and vice versa. Speaking towards this transition, Danielle Brathwaite-Shirley, the artist and archivist of the Black Trans Archive, an infinitely modifiable online archive that takes the form of an interactive video game, has heralded this moment as 'the end of passive art'.[1]

Alice Bucknell,
Still from *The Martian Word for World is Mother*,
2022

Spanning three speculative worlds set on Mars, this three-channel video uses game engines and artificial intelligence to survey humanity's complicated relationship to the Red Planet and the role that language plays in creating and destroying worlds.

 As virtual and physical spaces collapse into each other to produce a hybrid multispace, artists equipped with the latest advances in game engine technologies are radically transforming both the video game medium and its message. Through their innovative use of rendering software shared with the disciplines of architecture and design, these creatives are building worlds that grapple with the most complex conditions of the present. While architecture's concern with multispace has sometimes veered towards constructing virtual neoliberal realms for speculative finance – as seen in the work of Zaha Hadid Architects' Liberland Metaverse, or the eco smart city of NEOM in Saudi Arabia, both discussed below – artists like Cheng are using multispace as a testing ground for entwining ecology, technology and culture.

Artists Making New Worlds

Brandishing the latest capabilities of the powerful real-time rendering software Unity, one of several prominent engines used in video game design, Cheng's work bears traces of earlier creative experiments in virtual world-making. In 2009, multimedia artist Cao Fei released *RMB City* – a fictional Chinese city built inside the online virtual world Second Life. Throughout its three-year lifespan, the digital metropolis cultivated a heterogeneous cyber community from across the globe: artists and curators as well as curious netizens who had stumbled upon the project by chance. Acting under a temporary, self-assembled governance, *RMB City* hosted exhibitions, contests, virtual groundbreaking ceremonies and even mayoral inaugurations within its cyber city hall. Conceived during a time of rapid urban development in China, the prescient project stands as an early testament to the social and political potential of gamespace to cultivate new shared worlds.

Projected to become a $400 billion industry by 2028,[2] gaming can no longer be written off as the humble pastime of bored teenagers or the guilty pleasure of troubled misanthropes. Video games have come a long way in both style and substance since the first-person shooter game engine was unveiled in the late 1990s, and further still from the clunky 1980s arcade machines that preceded it. As graphic capabilities and narrative worlds grow ever more complex, gaming is proving increasingly capable of responding to the wicked problems defining the present: from the ecological crisis to economic meltdown and social inequalities.

One such example is the puzzle-platform game *Never Alone* (2014), developed by Upper One Games, the first Indigenous-owned video game company in the US. The game tells a tale of climate disaster and collaborative ecological survival through Indigenous knowledge and more-than-human perspectives (players swap between playing an Iñupiaq girl named Nuna and her Arctic fox companion). Another case lies in *Spiritfarer* (2020), a sandbox game released at the height of the Covid-19 pandemic's first wave. Players embody a chipper daughter-of-Charon with a previous life as a death doula, who must ferry a procession of more-than-human souls into the afterlife. Using a highly empathetic narrative and a pared-back, emotive graphic style, the game dexterously navigates complex issues of death, grief and mental health.

Cao Fei (Second Life avatar: China Tracy),
Still from *RMB City: A Second Life City Planning*,
2007

RMB City documents Fei's exercise in building a fictional Chinese city in the virtual world of Second Life in 2009. Players were invited to become part of the digital community, which featured its own art exhibitions, political system and public holidays.

Sahej Rahal,
Mythmachine,
Baltic Centre for Contemporary Art,
Gateshead, UK,
2022

Rahal's interactive work is an open-world video game that encourages players to commune with an AI-powered nonhuman intelligence. Players' movements are synthesised into an electronic score, a kind of multispecies language strategy that transcends traditional forms of understanding.

In a similar way, artists like Sahej Rahal, Jakob Kudsk Steensen and the members of the Keiken artist collective are leveraging gaming technologies to speculate on future entanglements of ecology, embodiment and cultural belief systems. Their practices engage with the climate crisis, the philosophy of technology and posthumanism, but use game engines and interactive gameplay to unpack these complex ideas in an accessible way.

Rahal's *Mythmachine* (2022) is drawn from the artist's ongoing interest in science-fiction and nonhuman intelligence as frameworks for reimagining the connections between music, the environment and folklore. The work's protagonists are spectral beings generated inside a game engine with the help of AI. Reacting to the player's motions in the virtual world, these creatures fuse song and movement to create a speculative shared language.

Meanwhile, Keiken's latest project, *Player of Cosmic ☙° Realms* (2022), contemplates the future of gameplay and embodiment in the metaverse. Comprised of *Bet(a) Bodies* – an interactive work featuring haptic wombs – and *The Life Game* – a playable CGI film – the work is installed as a futuristic lounge with seating areas that appear to float atop a bed of white sand. Players can don the artificial wombs to experience the frequencies and vibrations of different animals that communicate through ultrasound, including bats, dolphins and whales. Steensen's *Berl-Berl* (2021), presented by Berlin-based cultural organisation Light Art Space (LAS) inside the cavernous architecture of the infamous nightclub Berghain, is an immersive journey back in time to Berlin's swampy past. The work combines living artefacts 3D scanned from Berlin's adjacent wetlands and speculations on its historical swamp ecosystem, bringing visitors backwards and forwards in time through a pulsing virtual landscape of epic scale.

Multispace Architecture: Retrofitted Tech for the Neoliberal Apocalypse

Applications of this technology in architecture have so far yielded comparatively disappointing outputs, with the bulk of projects producing hypercapitalistic worlds dressed in new metaverse clothes. These visions range from Zaha Hadid Architects' virtual urban city of Liberland Metaverse, announced in 2022, to NEOM, Saudi Arabia's planned megacity in the desert. Brandished as the destination point for networking and financialisation of the emerging Web 3.0 economy, the online world of Liberland is a digital replica of a physical libertarian micronation, the Free Republic of Liberland – a sovereign state located within the disputed territory between Croatia and Serbia. Appearing like a glitzy seastead beached on the shores of late capitalism, Liberland's virtual campus, designed by Patrik Schumacher, is full of parametric curb appeal, its swooping pavilions and 'incubation zones' tempting tech bros to throw down crypto-capital in its accelerationist enterprise. By investing in the 'digital twin' of this micronation through purchasing pixelated plots of land in the metaverse, investors are guaranteed the same plots in the physical territory of Liberland. That is, once, and only if, it actually materialises.

A similar yet inverted strategy is being rolled out across the Arabian Peninsula, where NEOM, a $1 trillion eco smart city in the desert, is currently being conjured up by Saudi Arabia's crown prince, Mohammed bin Salman. Trumpeted as a 'civilizational revolution'[3] by its creators, NEOM's high-tech centrepiece, a 100-mile-long (160-kilometre) 'linear city' appropriately branded The Line, allegedly designed by the architectural office Morphosis, claims to 'protect and enhance' the natural environment of the desert yet does the exact opposite. NEOM seeks to dissolve itself into the desert landscape by restricting its human presence between the slivers of a mirrored façade; the insides of this reflective horizontal skyscraper will host a jacked-up version of nature including a vertical garden composed of 100 million native trees, glow-in-the-dark beaches, and even an artificial moon. Like Liberland, it pitches a 'digital twin' economic system (tax-free, of course); those who invest in the speculative property offered up in NEOM's residential district will also obtain financial resources and civic rights in the AI-powered governance of The Line (the only currency intended to be handled in the city is crypto).

Liberland and NEOM operate on a shared conceptual premise of delusional disruptor thinking, casting themselves as the radical innovators of the 21st century but replicating many of the previous centuries' techno-utopian fantasies. Both projects hype a hubristic vision of 'hypernature' – an artificially constructed environment engineered to outperform the natural world – and are pivoting in the exact opposite direction of degrowth that the architecture industry desperately needs to embrace in order to curtail its heavily polluting production model.

Liam Young,
Still from *Planet City*,
2021

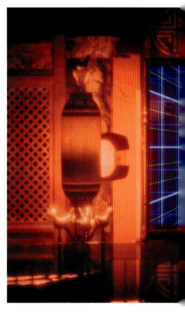

above: Speculative architect Young's project proposes urban design solutions to the increasingly urgent problem of overpopulation. Taking the form of a video work and multimedia installation, here showing the stacked farms of his *Planet City*, it offers a profound view into a global megacity capable of hosting the world's entire human population.

Ultimately, architecture's most high-profile engagements with virtual world-making currently appear more invested in accelerating social inequity and our impending climate doom than proposing any meaningful alternative.

Worlds of Exception in Multispace Architecture

Thankfully, there are also counter-narratives being produced within this space – and perhaps unsurprisingly, their creators are architects whose work veers into art practice. Film director and designer Liam Young's monumental *Planet City* (2021) is a film, virtual reality (VR) experience and book set in a speculative hyper-densified urban environment, where a global population of 10 billion people has relocated in order to surrender the Earth's remaining surface area to a new nature. Directly responding to the climate emergency through speculative fiction, the work applies a systems approach to the human-made crisis we are living through, suggesting an anti-apocalyptic counter-narrative based on collaboration. Melding utopian and dystopian elements, *Planet City* resists the techno-solutionist approach to future urban development that characterises projects like NEOM and Liberland.

Lawrence Lek,
Still from *AIDOL*,
2019

below: Lek is known for a cinematic body of work that traverses electronic music and virtual worlds. *AIDOL* – part of his *Sinofuturist Trilogy* – centres on the relationship between gaming, creativity, artificial intelligence, postcolonialism and the climate crisis.

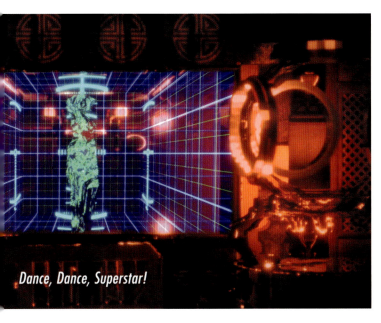

Alice Bucknell,
Still from *Swamp City*,
2021

Set in the Florida Everglades within a near-future reality of severe climate disruption, *Swamp City* explores the interconnections of technology, ecology, and lifestyle capitalism.

Similarly, the artist, filmmaker and musician Lawrence Lek – a graduate of the Architectural Association (AA) in London – uses a combination of virtual world-making, speculative storytelling and original scores to produce cinematic worlds that address the influence of technology on society, including the rise of AI and automated creativity, the cultural complexities of postcolonialism and what happens when reality itself becomes gamified. Lek's *Sinofuturist Trilogy* (2016–19) explores, through a dazzling trifecta of CGI films wrapped around his own soundtracks, the expired existentialism of a nation-state, climate meltdown, postcolonial independence and the dreams of an aspirational AI pop star. Like Young, Lek uses the latent space of game engines to design and prototype alternative visions for the future while unabashedly parsing the complex conditions of the present.

With projects that are so weak in concept and so inflated in image like NEOM and Liberland, what exactly can architects offer in the speculative space of the multiverse that artists, game designers and filmmakers cannot do better? Perhaps the answer lies in a shift of perspective, wherein architects might integrate their technical capacities for building at a systems scale with the novel approaches and outlooks developed by these other spatial practitioners.

Turning away from the half-baked propositions of starchitect-studded mixed-reality masterplans, we can better appreciate the rigour (and beauty) of the hybrid worlds made by artists and gamers today. This speculative practice of world-making lets us glimpse multiple possible futures that are within reach, sharing an approach with speculative fiction writers like Ursula K Le Guin and Octavia E Butler. These futures are resolutely anti-apocalyptic, non-dogmatic and open-ended in nature, much like the gaming ecosystems they embody. By playing as nonhuman characters, expanding our understanding of a world in nonlinear or geologic time, or tapping into voices or ideas erased from history, these imagined worlds help us come to terms with the many entangled crises defining the present. Whether you walk into a gallery or pick up the console at home, entering these environments is an exercise in imagining better futures, more equitable relationships from climate to culture, all brought to life in the latent worlds of multispace. ⌂

Notes
1. Danielle Brathwaite-Shirley, 'Archiving What Was Left Out', online talk given at NN Contemporary, Northampton, 20 October 2021: https://nncontemporaryart.org/events/danielle-brathwaite-shirley-archiving-what-was-left-out/.
2. Zion Market Research, *Global Gaming Market Report and Forecast*, February 2022.
3. NEOM website: https://www.neom.com/en-us/regions/theline.

Text © 2023 John Wiley & Sons Ltd. Images: pp 94–5 Courtesy of the artists and Julia Stoschek Collection; pp 96–7 © 2022 Ian Cheng. Presented by LAS (Light Art Space) © Andrea Rossetti; pp 98–9, 103(b) Courtesy of the artist; pp 100–01(b) Courtesy of the artist, Vitamin Creative Space and Sprüth Magers; p 101(t) © Sahej Rahal; p 102(t) © Liam Young; pp 102–03(c) © Lawrence Lek: AIDOL, 2019. Image courtesy Sadie Coles HQ, London

Micaela Mantegna and
Marcelo Rinesi

The Anti-Metaverse

WhoIsGallifrey / Micaela Mantegna,
Fauxtivity,
2023

Infinite possibilities do not guarantee diversity.

WhoIsGallifrey / Micaela Mantegna,
Doorspace,
2023

When space is essentially free, topology defines affordances and expresses ideology.

Multispace and the Intersections of Reality

Virtual spaces offer the incredible mix of opportunities and risks that are only available when designing a new universe (almost) from scratch. Arguing that these spaces are just as real as the 'real world', **Micaela Mantegna and Marcelo Rinesi** point out that architects are obligated to share their intellectual and visualising skills beyond the discipline to give more of humanity the possibility of operating in their own multispatial environments, and in so doing taking the legislation of space away from the neoliberal few.

There is a deep-rooted bias against the digital; intangible goods, relationships and spaces are seen as something less valuable than their tangible counterparts. Internet friends are not 'real friends', much like ebooks 'are just not the same' as books.

Maybe this is rooted in a collectively learned empiricist human instinct that links persistence and tangibility with value, signalling something that can be appropriated. Either way, digital spaces are frequently demoted due to their perceived ephemeral and intangible nature. They exist as long as we can access them – the computer's lights are on, the servers are running and the gatekeeper's fee has been paid – and much like the sound of the tree falling in the forest, can we be sure they persist when we are not looking at them?

In defence of digital spaces, it is clear this set of assumptions does not survive unscathed through a more thorough analysis. Sandcastles or ice sculptures are also fragile and destined to exist only within the confines of a limited timeframe, but that does not mean these structures are less 'real'. Cloud computing has challenged definitions of value by enabling ubiquitous access as something far more relevant than information confined to a single device.

It is true that access to digital spaces is a mediated experience: hardware devices like computers or headsets, together with servers and software, enable connection and digital architecture for the structure. However, this could also be said of any 'real' place that is not within walking distance, or that is privately owned. Our access to said spaces is restricted either by another medium (car, train, aeroplane) or by another gatekeeper (owner, business hours, etc).

To understand the emerging notion of multispace, we need to overcome this binary notion of the digital and the tangible as opposing realities. We have been trained to think about virtual and physical spaces as a binary, when they are actually a continuum with many intersections of reality. There is no more online/offline distinction, life entangles both aspects, and the experiences are pervasive, carrying on from one to the other.

Frequently we hear that digital spaces are not 'real', with their value as venues for experiences and relationships intrinsically suspect. But though they are 'artificially created', they are just as real as the 'real world', as something that can be perceived through our senses and impacts us. Digital experiences have lingering effects in our cognition that transcend their native boundaries, remaining beyond the act of taking away the headset or closing down a Zoom call.

WhoIsGallifrey /
Micaela Mantegna,
Innerspace Site,
2023

Site constraints in multispace are
conceptual, not physical.

Creating Infinity, Then Taming It

In our current internet-enabled society and the future trajectory of multispace, human experience happens in a 'reality gradient'[1] that blends overlapping perceptions and different amounts of artificial and natural, organic and designed, digital and tangible.

The term 'extended reality' (XR) has been coined to cover different technological implementations and ways to experience virtual content, either as superimposed layers of digital information on top of tangible reality (augmented reality – AR), a complete occlusion and replacement (virtual reality – VR) or hybrid environments allowing manipulation of digital objects (mixed reality – MR).

The 'magic circle' has been shattered; realities are not separate compartments, but intersecting spectra of experiences blending digital and analogue in ways that will become even more indistinguishable.

Multispace's potential for newness, of course, far outstrips that of purely physical – or, for that matter, purely digital – environments. In virtual reality, for instance, the basic laws of the universe as we experience it – including basic assumptions like the structure of distance, common physics, perception of colours, the way senses work, etc – have to be

> **Digital experiences have lingering effects in our cognition that transcend their native boundaries, remaining beyond the act of taking away the headset or closing down a Zoom call**

painstakingly implemented by sophisticated software and hardware. Architecture moves from using space as infrastructure to becoming the infrastructure of space.

Distance, presence, perception and even randomness are no less things to be built, maintained, controlled and charged for than are amenities in a building or a private park. How are we to preserve serendipity and the spontaneous unpredictability that is truly integral to human experience, when it is simulated and therefore artificial?

Perhaps an even deeper question should be: why are we so eager to hardwire scarcity and reproduce the restraints of the tangible world in a medium that is essentially limitless? In digital spaces, there is no artificial air to breath, and neither is there the need for form to follow function. The aesthetics of objects are no longer tied to their functionality, nor to any laws of physics that are not coded into a space.

Likewise, the economics of building a digital space are not tied to the cost of materials or sometimes even labour (with the advancement of generative AI). And when a texture, object or asset is developed, it could potentially be replicated infinitely at almost no cost, and even delivered across the world without the need to factor in the expense of supply chains or intermediaries.

The possibilities that digital spaces and abundance technologies are opening up are a direct challenge to a capitalist system built on scarcity. Charging money for a plot of land that could potentially be infinite is just digital feudalism.

WhoIsGallifrey /
Micaela Mantegna,
Seeing Like A Space,
2023

Corporate architecture is not built to be seen but to see.

The directions we travel in when faced by these dilemmas are what distinguishes multispace from 'the metaverse'; where the former conceives the 'blendedness' of physical and digital realities in terms of openness, equality and decentralisation, the latter leads to a world that is closed, controlled and very often corporate.

The metaverse's financialisation and privatisation of the laws of physics dramatises and deepens the financialisation and privatisation of other aspects of our shared world. Object persistence becomes no more reliable than any other content protected by intellectual property laws, terms of service or cloud service. In the metaverse, physics is on a freemium model. Each layer and area in the metaverse comes with its own corporate landlord/demiurge. No wonder there is so much being bet on making us move there.

> Freedom of movement between competing spacetime corporate authoritarian layers and areas of the metaverse would be a thin foundation for a better society

The One-Way Magic Door

Initiatives to make digital spaces a more viable context for more appealing societies involve mechanisms for ensuring the portability of avatars, assets and interpersonal networks. This is in a way a multiversal counterpart to similar EU rules for freedom of work, movement and financial transactions. As such, they are plausibly necessary but ultimately insufficient ways to guarantee minimum rights: the libertarian postulate that freedom of choice guarantees good options only works when barriers of entry are low enough to allow for non-oligopoly competition, something we already know is far from guaranteed when it comes to large-scale computing environments.

Freedom of movement between competing spacetime corporate authoritarian layers and areas of the metaverse would be a thin foundation for a better society.

A key observation based on similar battles won, lost and still being fought is that the key resource is often not technology but skilled imagination and focal points. It is nearly as easy to obtain a personal domain and set up an independent blog as it is to create and use an account in a social network (and would certainly become even easier to do given sufficient demand), and the long-term advantages in terms of independence, control and possibilities are infinitely larger.

Despite this, the personal website is no longer the default online footprint of an individual, or sometimes even a company. This is because, firstly, creating one is not something that we are encouraged to think of as possible, or taught to do; and, secondly, because even across social and practice groups – including professional and academic groups – where the long-term value of self-controlled communication and collaboration networks outside corporate control is even more critical (and in fact is the historical basis of the possibility of such disciplines and activities), there is little or no internal pressure or incentive to do so.

You can own a mansion in the middle of nowhere, or for the same money, a crowded apartment in the middle of a megalopolis. The value (and the network effects) comes from being where everyone is, and that is what is taken advantage of to (re)centralise the decentralised premise of the metaverse. Because even in a world of digital abundance and digital twins, human attention is *the* scarce resource.

A key approach to understanding the stakes and strategies at play in an ongoing competition best described as a land grab in territories yet to be created is to look at what prerogatives the would-be architects of digital spaces keep for themselves. Movement *within* a single owner's area of the metaverse, interactions through their communication tools, and the creation of content, ephemeral or not, using their tools and systems, are allowed and encouraged. But moving things *out*, to somebody else's area of the metaverse or to the physical world, is the most heavily policed and punished activity.

WhoIsGallifrey /
Micaela Mantegna,
Public Domain Spolia, 2023

The entire history of architectural reality and fantasy are available in
multispace; why rebuild skyscrapers and theme parks?

WhoIsGallifrey /
Micaela Mantegna,
Topology of Surveillance,
2023

When the abyss gazes at you, will you gaze back?

WhoIsGallifrey /
Micaela Mantegna,
The Complexity Vortex,
2023

Free of regulatory and physical constraints, the asymptotic endpoint
of oligopoly-driven architecture is exactly the same as its beginning.
This is by design.

This is a familiar pattern among internet behemoths, particularly when it comes to creation and interpersonal relationships. It is easy to publish on Amazon, but criminal to create a pdf file of a book to send to a friend. You can link to anywhere *from* a Facebook post, but they are extremely resistant to reuse from elsewhere. And your most valuable 'asset' in those spaces, the network of relationships of interest or trust reified as a set of links between accounts representing individuals and organisations that (most of the time) are not themselves those accounts, is in fact the most difficult, or rather impossible, thing to metaphorically put in a suitcase and run away with.

Access control – the way areas of the metaverse monitor and shape the flow of identity, information and creativity between each other and with the physical world – will never be merely a differentiating feature or focused on who or what can get in. Its goal is to keep whatever is valuable inside by entangling it with proprietary technical and symbolic infrastructures and refusing to make it practical to move it elsewhere. The keystone of the economic logic of any multispace with limited data ownership is bait-and-switch, or rather hostage-taking.

Architecture as Guerrilla World-Building

Architecture as a discipline is not necessarily a better example than most, but it has the intellectual and social tools to help limit the same sort of semi-centralised control, financialisation and cultural de-diversification that characterises the metaverse and has already soured its physical and digital parents.

As a community of practice, architecture can – and should, and must – conceptualise, build, test and make visible the tools and processes of multispace-building as a way to counter the dominance of metaversal digital spaces. Societies, to a degree, are aware of past and future architectural possibilities because architects draw, render, model and build more often and more diversely than required by pure financial logic. The fact that digital spaces can be as multiple and varied in scale, aspect and function as we might need or want, will be at most an abstract reminder from technologists – unless, that is, research, architects and urbanists fully take advantage of these possibilities not just in business or research-as-business projects (as per the metaverse), but in personal projects, group hangouts and even momentary whims.

WhoIsGallifrey /
Micaela Mantegna,
Everything and Everywhere, All At Once,
2023

True freedom in a multispace does not mean 'choose whichever you want' but 'build whatever you can imagine'.

But keeping alive the awareness of possibility will not be enough. Architecture also has the responsibility of teaching these skills beyond the discipline itself. There are good practical reasons why amateurs are not allowed to build bridges, but on the other hand, while professional interior designers are expected to be more proficient than amateurs, we do not forbid people from shaping and decorating their own spaces whenever and however they wish: the freedom to do so, and the psychological and even existential benefits of it, far outweigh the professional or aesthetic advantages of a formal or informal monopoly.

If the metaverse constitutes a network of corporate parks, multispace exists as an organic grid of infinitely nested personal spaces. Architects, in their most general ability to imagine and create spaces, must not only show people this by constant example, but also teach, in every formal and informal way, how to do it. Digital spaces can only be liveable when they are both communal and personal. They can only fulfil their potential when every inhabitant is also a creator, not in the shallow sense of posting new 'content' to maintain the fragile financial viability of dubiously useful corporate infrastructures, but in the most meaningful one of deeply influencing their own lives in a way that may also enrich other people's.

Embracing and developing the concept and practice of multispace is a vital means for us to do this, helping us counter the ways this new arena with new possibilities is already being fenced by many of the same actors that have fenced and strip-mined those of previous ones. Activism and regulation, but also imagination and shared skill, are the tools that will determine the multispatial world and what sort of society will live there. ⌓

Note
1. Micaela Mantegna, 'Diving Decompression and VR Aftercare', *Medium,* 14 February 2023: https://abogamer.medium.com/diving-decompression-and-vr-aftercare-5da6184ed8ad.

Text © 2023 John Wiley & Sons Ltd.
Images © Micaela Mantegna / WhoIsGallifrey.
AI-generated images created in DALL·E

All At Once – From Zoom Fatigue to Immersive Digital Experiences

Why Architecture Must Adapt

iheartblob,
Tales from _Spaces,
2021

A visualisation of part of *_Spaces,* a decentralised virtual city. The project offers a unique perspective on how we perceive and interact with urban spaces, providing a platform for exploring alternative approaches to city planning and design.

The constellation of digital techniques, software, visual and haptic prosthetics is growing exponentially by the day. Such innovations allow all manner of choreographed synthesis between the world we see, unaugmented, and the world we experience through our devices. With her practice iheartblob, Sasha Belitskaja makes Surrealist architectonic interventions and installations that straddle the virtual/actual divide, using the best of both worlds.

Architects are not prepared for multispace. In our daily lives we traverse digital landscapes, with our identities defined by which platform or space we are inhabiting. We exist across platforms, co-inhabiting multiple spaces all at once: listening to a podcast whilst scrolling through social media feeds and virtually inhabiting spatialised work environments, navigating multiple data-streams simultaneously, seamlessly fluctuating between focused engagement and passive background involvement.

Unlike our physical selves, in multispace we have the flexibility to shift personas, remaking our digital presence as we see fit, constantly fluid and adaptable. We can create and maintain many digital identities through which we participate across, within and through diverse ecosystems and control our own anonymity. We are entering a moment where the 2D digital worlds we inhabit are no longer enough; we demand a spatial connectedness across devices, across platforms, across identities. Architecture is well positioned but ill equipped to define this spatialised, immersive web of identity and experience.

Unlocking the Potential of the Spatialised Multispace
The Covid-19 pandemic accelerated the emergence and understanding of multispace as an inevitable development in human interaction. With the sudden shift to remote work, online learning and virtual socialising, people adapted to using digital tools for almost all aspects of their lives. Although spending a lot of time with 2D screens has helped usher in the blurring of physical and digital space, we now see the negative impact of flattened spatial experience with the emergence of the likes of Zoom fatigue. From a purely technological point of view, these tools were not yet ready for the level of reliance placed on them, nor was there much, if any consideration of the role within a broader field of human interaction.

Cognitively we are used to engaging with a variety of physical spaces. But in the digital world, for the most part we are limited to flattened experiences which confine themselves to user-interface (UI) or user-experience (UX) standards; only rarely do we have variety, and we certainly do not experience spatiality. At least for now. Already there are spatial computing tools available for designers – architects or otherwise – to harness. Yet where they are being deployed, this is frequently done in isolation, without considering the multispatial lives we now lead and how we look to connect and express ourselves with the authority of the digital but with the familiarity of the physical.

Ownership of Digital Space
Over the last seven years, the extended-reality architecture studio iheartblob has explored how architecture can overlap with the digital and, through this, begun to outline an approach to a multitude of digital connectedness across fully immersive to mixed-reality (MR) experiences. When working across these domains, it is important to balance novelty with familiarity. These experiences offer limitless interactions with an immersive world, but they must feel like a natural extension to our identity. To spatialise these

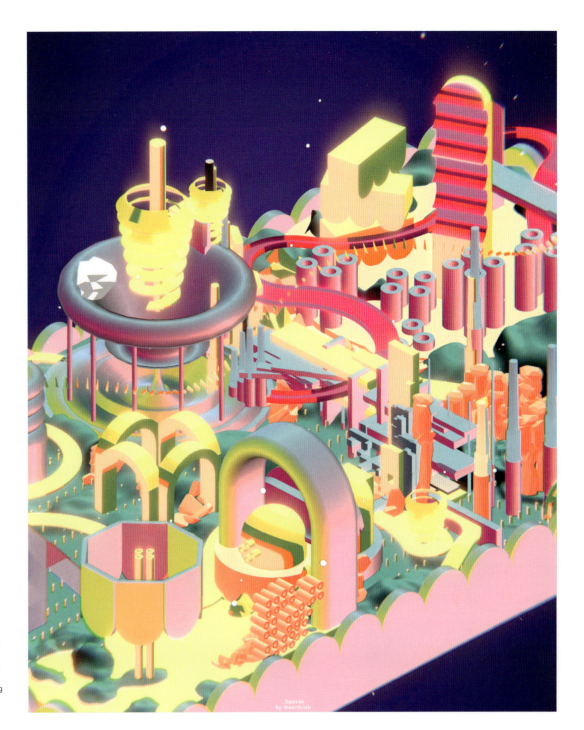

iheartblob,
_Spaces NFT,
2021

Axonometric drawing of _Spaces, showing an overview of the decentralised city and showcasing the numerous pavilions, walkways and structures that visitors can explore within the immersive digital environment. Through its colourful aesthetics, _Spaces offers a glimpse into a future where architecture and digital technology converge, creating opportunities for community-driven design and virtual experiences.

interactions, iheartblob has been exploring various levels of immersion from the scale of an installation to that of a city, as in the case of _Spaces – the first fully immersive, decentralised virtual city.

_Spaces was designed and minted by iheartblob in 2021 and exhibited at A+D Museum, Los Angeles. The project was inspired by the lack of immersive spaces at the start of the pandemic, and by ideas of spatialising everyday internet usage alongside the familiar homescreen app workflow. The city was filled with familiar architectural forms; arches and columns are juxtaposed by looping animations, with colourful textures and spatially aware sounds to enhance spatial presence.

The immersive space plays an important role of defining new concepts of authorship and ownership. By engaging with a decentralised process which utilised smart contracts – self-executing agreements written in code – to define boundaries, the team was able to work outside the confines of regulatory standards, and design an architecture than can be for the community and funded by the community. The project repositions how architecture and the virtual should consider each other, providing a route towards architecture which challenges the status quo of how architecture is designed, organised and funded.

Embracing the Phygital

The freedom afforded by virtual spaces can be exhilarating but there is equal enthusiasm to be found by dialling down immersion in a mixing of realities where the immersion overlays and interacts with our own physical environment. *ARc de Blob*, an MR pavilion built for the 2021 edition of the Winter Stations international design competition in Toronto, Canada, explores the potential of a future where physical and digital objects coexist. The pavilion is a colourful 'phygital' (physical-digital) landmark: a point of orientation, interaction and refuge. The arch acts as a frame for a virtual portal/refuge seen in MR – a space of new digital worlds designed to encourage visitors to play and interact together both digitally and physically. In this way, the piece explores the potential for an evolving mix of digital art and physical architecture to create playful interactions between these realities.

By embracing the dynamic and real-time nature of digital forms, MR can be utilised as a liminal scanner that provides a window for integrating movement, colour and interaction into the built form. Combining elements across the physical and digital worlds creates unique spatial opportunities that cannot be replicated by either medium alone – which is what is meant by 'phygital'. Coupled with potential for hybrid personal expression, such spaces provide tangible experiences where our digital identities can interact across our physical cities.

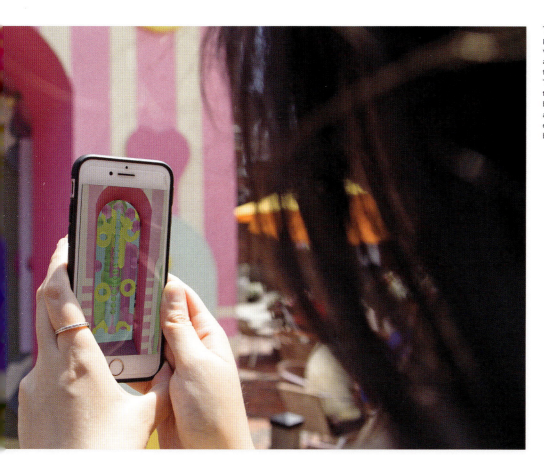

The arch acts as a frame for a virtual portal or refuge in MR, providing visitors with opportunities to play and interact in creative environments that merge physical and digital space. The virtual environment is designed to encourage playful interactions between visitors, both digitally and physically, creating a shared experience that blends the boundaries between the real and the virtual.

`iheartblob,
ARc de Blob,
Winter Stations,
Toronto,
Canada,
2021`

opposite: This architectural object, made for the annual Winter Stations design competition, mixes together materials and colour with the ability to interact digitally and connect through a mixed-reality (MR) app.

right: ARc de Blob takes the standalone, traditional architectural platonic form of the arch and flips its appropriated narrative, reclaiming its nature as an architectural default. Its ornamentation reflects on the crisis of digital translation, 2D to 3D, classical to present.

iheartblob,
Fungible/Non-Fungible Pavilion,
Tallinn Architecture Biennale (TAB),
Tallinn, Estonia,
2022

The components of the installation are not only physical parts of the structure but also serve as direct representations of the non-fungible token (NFT) objects that were designed and minted by the community. This process enabled a decentralised design approach that allowed for more inclusivity and community ownership.

Decentralising for Community Design

When it comes to expressing ourselves virtually and defining our spatial presence within our homes, cities and worlds, the use of tools such as augmented reality (AR), virtual reality (VR), blockchains and others is crucial. Immersive technologies offer agency – agency to define our surroundings and allow ourselves to both connect and contribute to the world around us without the forceful hand of individual stakeholders or budgeting clients. This is in stark contrast to the hierarchical nature of the architecture profession which often results in designs that cater to the narrow focus of stakeholders, leading to replication of designs and neglecting the needs of those who actually inhabit what is being realised. Decentralisation, which these tools offer, allows a unique way forward for a more inclusive and sustainable design process, transferring ownership of design to all and providing agency to communities.

The *Fungible/Non-Fungible Pavilion* is an example of this in practice – the first physical pavilion designed, constructed and funded using non-fungible tokens (NFTs), a form of digital assets stored and verified on digital ledgers known as blockchains. The project was created as part of the Tallinn Architecture Biennale in Estonia in 2022. The pavilion was co-designed, co-funded and co-owned by the community. Utilising NFTs allowed anyone to contribute to both the design and funding for the construction of the pavilion by designing and minting their own block. This community-oriented design model allows for as many participants as possible, making the pavilion as large as the participants determine. People around the world designed and contributed through a virtual 3D environment, with each block defined in terms of its authorship and ownership while also contributing collectively to the whole. As built, each block has a near-field communication (NFC) tag, allowing visitors to tap the NFC with a mobile device and receive the verifiable information, including the owner, designer and price, alongside a 3D model for a distributed architectural documentation.

Across all of these technologies, architects can play a defining role in articulating the relationship between digital objects and spaces and their physical counterparts. Decentralised community design processes offer new, inclusive and democratic ways of designing that have the potential to shape or reshape not just the digital world, but the physical one too.

top: In order to create the world's first NFT pavilion, iheartblob (pictured in the image) developed an NFT-generative tool that enables anyone to design and mint objects. Each NFT generated through the tool funded a unique physical twin, which is now incorporated into the pavilion.

bottom: To access metadata of each timber block, visitors can use their smartphone to scan the circular near-field communication (NFC) tag located on each block. This will provide information of the piece, including the owner, designer and a 3D model for a distributed architectural documentation.

Across all of these technologies the architect can play a defining role in articulating the relationship between digital objects and spaces and their physical counterparts

The Age of AI Co-pilot Design

In recent years, artificial intelligence (AI) has become increasingly prevalent in the field of architecture, presenting both opportunities and challenges for architects. Using AI to help design enables designers to work more efficiently and generate ideas at a faster pace. Generative tools such as ChatGPT and Midjourney can expand and speed up architects' capabilities by providing them with various text and visual options to solve design problems. The merging of different images to create an infinite number of design possibilities can be especially helpful in overcoming creative blocks and generating fresh, innovative designs.

In addition to improving the design process of physical buildings, AI also holds great potential when designing multispatial structures, systems and processes. With the rise of data-driven, personalised environments, we are in need of fast and infinitely customisable design solutions for how this can be reflected spatially. AI has the potential to enable architects to generate designs that are themselves unique and tailored to the unique constantly changing requirements, providing a more personalised and real-time experience of space generation.

Being able to maintain and create multiple layers of presence across fully virtual and mixed reality in these ways lays the groundwork for designing spaces that can encourage flexible identity, while contributing to functional, accessible, comfortable environments defined by people's needs. All of this heralds the possibility of new immersive spaces of knowledge and interconnectedness, which allow people from all over the world to seamlessly connect and interact, leading to new opportunities for education, entertainment, socialising and commerce.

However, the potential for addiction, privacy violations and mental health issues associated with technology and social media cannot be ignored. The systems that underpin these spaces must be designed carefully and thoughtfully, ensuring that people are not replaced by their digital avatars, and that virtual experiences do not become a substitute for physical-life experiences and relationships. Much work remains to be done. Every entity that exists today on the internet has the potential of becoming a spatial experience dialled in and out across the real world of tomorrow, with some entities requiring full immersion and others occupying our world as spatial notifications. The fundamental ways we interact with the digital world and built environment through these technologies is, however, yet to be designed, presenting a massive challenge but also an opportunity.

`iheartblob,`
`Fungible ARc,`
`2023`

above: An AI-generated design created by blending visuals from *ARc de Blob* and the *Fungible / Non-Fungible Pavilion*. This highlights the potential for AI to expand architects' capabilities and generate fresh, innovative designs by merging different images to create an infinite number of design possibilities from existing projects.

opposite: AI-generated designs created from two images are stylistically similar to both inputs but providing various design proposals.

We now navigate spaces where our physical and digital experience are constantly in flux and where our experience and identity are continually being mediated

Multispatial Architecture

Architecture is well positioned and well equipped to define this spatialised, immersive web of identity and experience. As this article has explored, immersive technologies, including VR and AR and others under the banner of Web 3.0, provide architects with the opportunity to define and augment the hybrid, multispatial environments we are increasingly inhabiting in real time. Moreover, decentralisation allows architects and communities to work for each other, not as the middle person between stakeholder goals and community ambition. Through the use of smart contracts and NFTs, architects can shape their own briefs and agendas, drive innovation within 'phygital' environments, create reconfigurable urban spaces and integrate traditional architectural design processes within custom experiences deployed online.

Our understanding and experience of space has shifted. We now navigate spaces where our physical and digital experience are constantly in flux and where our experience and identity are continually being mediated. As we hurtle towards the increasingly complex and interconnected world of multispaces, we must create more seamless integrations and transitions between physical and digital spaces. We must consider how this can enhance and enrich our physical world and our digital existence within it, all of which requires a fundamental shift in the ways we approach design. This means moving away from the traditional boundaries of physical architecture and towards a more holistic approach that incorporates digital and virtual spaces together, where architecture becomes a decentralised collaborative process focused on creating fully immersive experiences – digital, physical and both. ᴅ

Text © 2023 John Wiley & Sons Ltd. Images: pp 113, 115 © iheartblob; pp 116(b), 117(b) © Khristel Stecher; pp 116–17(t) Photo by Jonathan Sabeniano, 2021; pp 118–19 ©Tõnu Tunnel; pp 120–21 © iheartblob. AI-generated images created in Midjourney

Owen Hopkins

SHIFTING CONTEXTS

LIAM YOUNG'S PROTOTYPES OF ARCHITECTURAL FUTURES

Digital technologies and visualisation techniques are changing the site(s) of architecture, as well as the notion of context and how architecture responds to it. In an interview with Guest-Editor **Owen Hopkins**, architect and filmmaker Liam Young discusses the shifting nature of 'site', architecture's possible futures and the centrality of speculation for the profession.

Liam Young,
Still from
The Great Endeavor,
2023

page 122: Reaching climate targets relies not just on slashing emissions, but also on developing the capacity to remove carbon dioxide from the atmosphere and storing it underground at the gigatonne scale. The scale of human extinction necessitates an infrastructural project mobilising labour, resources and international cooperation on a planetary scale at a complexity never before achieved. VFX supervisor: Alexey Marfin.

Liam Young,
Still from
Choreographic Camouflage,
2021

page 123: The dance performance and film present a new vocabulary of movement that Young designed, in collaboration with choreographer Jacob Jonas, to disguise the proportions of someone's body from the skeleton detection algorithms used by modern city-surveillance networks to track and identify individuals.

Liam Young,
Still from *Renderlands*,
2019

below: This mixed-reality film is set in the outsourced video-game companies and render farms of India. A render-farm worker has fallen in love with the digital model of a beautiful Hollywood actress after spending his 14 hours a day endlessly rotoscoping, rendering and compositing her into blockbuster films.

Architects have always sought to visualise the future. In many ways, it is inherent to the discipline. After all, to design is to imagine something that doesn't yet exist that through that process brings it into being. And for centuries architecture has functioned as a tool for imagining future worlds, whether they end up in physical form or simply as speculation.

Among the best known imagineers working today is Liam Young, renowned internationally for his films that envisage radical urban futures, technological transformations and environmental ruptures. What makes Young's work stand out even more is that despite this long history of architects imagining the future, the vast majority today have seemingly forgotten how to do it.

'There are times when making and shaping physical buildings is extraordinarily urgent', says Young, and 'then there are other points in time when, actually, the most viable thing we could do as architects is make a drawing, where speculative projects become more fundamental. I think we're in a moment like that now, a moment when technology is arriving at us faster than our cultural and social understandings of what it might mean.'

Architects, Young argues, have a vital role to play in helping us catch up, by 'prototyping the possible futures that these emerging technologies might be setting in motion as a means to help us to understand which systems we should be embracing and which we should be running away from screaming'.

While seemingly outside of architecture's traditional orbit, for Young this type of work is actually a continuation of what architects have always done: 'I trained as an architect in Australia where architecture really has one narrative, which is site specificity. In a context where the environment, the weather, the location is so extraordinary, it's difficult to imagine other roles that architecture plays other than relating to responding to that context. That was my training and I guess in many ways I'm still doing that. I'm still exploring what site means in a context where site is ever shifting.'

Expanded Sites

Today, a site is no longer simply a question of topography and of social and cultural relations enacted through physical proximities. 'We live amidst a networked ecology the size of the planet,' says Young. 'Everything somehow is connected to everything, and we're all traversing on these very intricate tendrils and networks which stretch all over the world. My move towards film was really about looking for a medium beyond the conventional site drawing that would help to deal with the spatial and temporal conditions of this new kind of site that we're engaging with.'

Despite this fundamental shift in something so fundamental to architecture as site, those very few architects who do work in these new, expanded contexts are usually seen as peripheral to the profession. 'I would argue,' Young counters, 'that they're firmly in the centre, that the people clinging on to working in a traditional office as a service industry, making buildings for rich clients, they're actually the people on the margins. The discipline just hasn't yet come to terms with this shift.'

Liam Young,
Still from *In the Robot Skies*,
2018

Written by Tim Maughan, the *In the Robot Skies* narrative was shot entirely through autonomous drones. From the eyes of the drones we see two teenagers each held by police order within the digital confines of their own council-estate tower block in London. In this near-future city, drones form agents of state surveillance but also become co-opted as the aerial vehicles through which two teens fall in love.

It is a mindset that is ingrained early on: 'I always talk about how in the last few years of architecture school you have professional practice class. It's the class that everyone dreads where they talk to you about liability and things like that. But this should be the most radical class in the entire school where the extraordinary knowledge you've acquired can be put to the test: where you develop new models of practice and start to define what you want to be doing as an architect and whether or not you want to be working in physical space or digital space.'

Instead, so much of the architectural debate about reshaping the profession and regaining lost agency frequently looks back (via some very rose-tinted glasses) to the postwar era when architecture was the pre-eminent discipline for effecting social change. Where radical or avant-garde architecture has existed in recent decades, it has 'really been in the service of luxury, creating shiny things for despots. To say that architects have a key role in the shaping and making of the world that we inhabit is hopeful at best.' Embracing the digital is, Young argues, a way to change this: 'Technologies have all moved towards us as spatial designers. Rather than diminishing our agency, I actually think that getting involved in designing digital worlds that a lot of people spend just as much time inhabiting as they do the real world allows us to strengthen what we do as architects. I think it's an extraordinary opportunity and architects are the best placed of any discipline to take it.'

Liam Young,
Still from *Where the City Can't See*, 2019

opposite: Written by Tim Maughan, *Where the City Can't See* is set in the Detroit Economic Zone (DEZ) and shot with the same scanning technologies used in autonomous vehicles. We see a group of young ravers drift through the smart-city point clouds in a driverless taxi. Adorned in machine-vision camouflage and anti-facial recognition tribal masks, they enact their escapist fantasies in the hidden spaces of the city.

Liam Young,
Still from *New City: Taobao Village,* 2019

below: Directed and designed by Young with VFX supervisor Alexey Marfin, *New City* is a series of skylines depicting a speculative urbanism, an exaggerated version of the present, in which we can project new cultural trends, environmental, political and economic forces. This New City skyline reimagines the contemporary Chinese phenomena of Taobao Villages as a hyper-dense urban region built entirely around the economies of the internet shopping giant.

Building New Worlds

Architects' contribution to shaping these spaces is vital not just for their own profession, but ultimately for the people who will inhabit the new worlds being created: 'When we make physical space in cities, it's not just a free-for-all; there are rules and laws that have been defined by some kind of democratically elected government. Now we're in a situation where the rules that govern the platforms of the digital world are often defined by a guy in a hoodie and sneakers or a narcissistic billionaire. There's a desperate need for architects-as-politicians or architects-as-advisors to think about the regulatory frameworks of these new spatial technologies. What are the different ways that we can start to create multiple metaverses as opposed to ending up with four metaverses, one owned by Google, one owned by Apple, one owned by Facebook, one owned by Amazon? How can we create a distributed platform that leads to more equitable online networks, digital spaces and environments?'

Technology is already reshaping the public sphere and public discourse – indeed, the very notion of what is public and what isn't. Yet, as Young is keen to stress, 'technology is totally agnostic and ambivalent. There's no inherently good or bad technology. Technology is just an extension of ourselves. It exaggerates the same contradictions and frailties that already exist within us.'

All this leaves us standing at a crossroads. Do we want to continue down the current path and let technology accentuate our worst traits and characteristics, and drive us further apart? Or do we try to take another road where we embrace technology's extraordinary possibilities for enabling new kinds of creativity, individuality and social interaction without letting it destroy the things that bind us together?

To take the right path we need those who can show the way – and architects, who represent a profession that even today is still defined by its belief in the possibility of building a more open, more equitable future, need to take the lead: 'For architects to not be designing and making these new digital worlds is negligent; at the very least it's a missed opportunity. It's our responsibility to get involved rather than try to eke out the last embers of a dying profession. I hope this issue is a call to arms for architects and students of architecture to get excited and to start working in this space.' ᗪ

All quotes in this article are from a video-call interview with the author on 27 February 2023.

Text © 2023 John Wiley & Sons Ltd.
Images © Liam Young

FROM ANOTHER PERSPECTIVE

A Word from △D Editor Neil Spiller

Ben Kelly Design, The Haçienda, Manchester, UK, 1982

Kelly's interior exhibits little of the cool, white, clean and neat doctrines that he would have been taught at the Royal College of Art (RCA). Instead it has an expedient aesthetic rejoicing in industrial materials and resilient finishes.

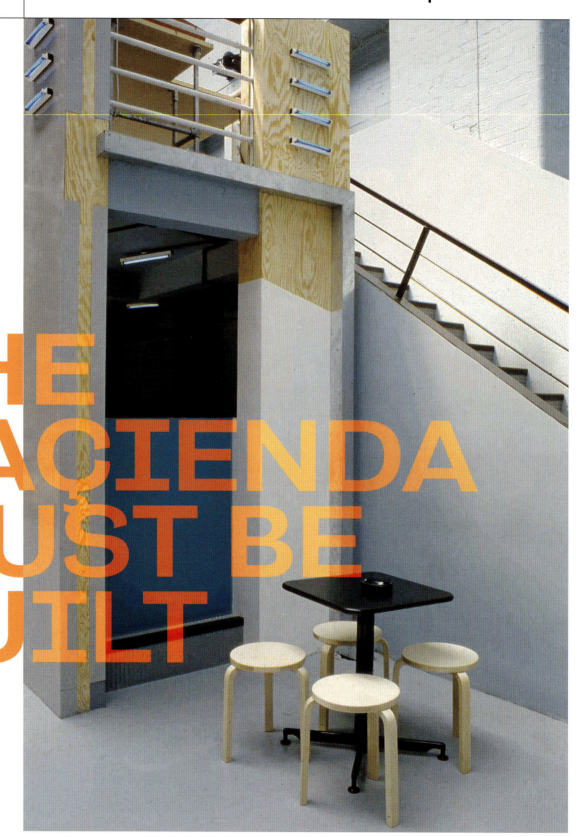

THE HAÇIENDA MUST BE BUILT

128

All cities are geological ... We move within a *closed* landscape whose landmarks constantly draw us towards the past. Certain *shifting* angles, certain *receding* perspectives, allow us to glimpse original conceptions of space, but this vision remains fragmentary. It must be sought in the magical locales.
— Ivan Chtcheglov, 'Formulary for a New Urbanism', 1953[1]

A magical locale for many was The Haçienda nightclub, which opened in 1982 in Manchester – a haven for post-punk, indie-music, acid-house and rave culture and a nexus for the musically inclined young of the area. Today, it has a mythical status perhaps propagated by its disappearance due to demolition in 1997. The idea for the club was conceived by the band New Order and their manager Rob Gretton. It was funded in part by them and in part by music moguls Alan Erasmus and Tony Wilson, co-founders with graphic designer and art director Peter Saville of the then nascent Factory Records (founded 1978). Ben Kelly designed the artistic interiors that gave it its iconic ambience.

Kelly grew up in a small village in the Yorkshire Dales called Appletreewick. Even in this quiet and unassuming hamlet, the wonder of rock and pop music had insinuated itself into the environs. Kelly describes himself as 'rubbish at school, more interested in the top 20 music chart than chemical equations'.[2] So at a little over 16 years old he enrolled at Lancaster Art School, in 1966, convinced it was an ideal environment within which he could grow his hair, wear what he liked, indulge his interest in the Rolling Stones, The Beatles etc, and be creatively experimental without conservative judgement. He graduated from Lancaster in 1970. The lure of London beckoned.

London Calling
Kelly joined the Royal College of Art (RCA) Interior Design course in the autumn of 1971. Its head was Sir Hugh Casson, the former Director of Architecture for the 1951 Festival Of Britain. Although all his tutors were architects, Kelly did not want to be an architect but a creator of 'art interiors'. Kelly describes himself as 'an oddball' at the RCA. The college was an exciting melting pot, with students experimenting with Pop Art, Minimalism, Land Art and Fashion. Among other influences on the young Kelly was the work of architect and interior designer Max Clendinning, whose oeuvre consisted of all-white interiors and other projects with bold colours and who in a Pop Art way deconstructed interior surfaces, furniture and fittings, a favourite example being the Islington house he shared with his partner Ralph Adron, a painter and theatre set designer. Both are known for their eclectic and iconoclastic work. This is where the notion of the 'art interior' came from, and their work has been the subject of a lifelong appreciation and inspiration for Kelly.

Ben Kelly Design, HOWIE shopfront, Covent Garden, London, 1976

It was with this small project that Kelly was to first make a name for himself, with its diagonal fenestration and perforated metal elements.

The early 1970s were heady times: The Who with their pop art targets on clothes, Andy Warhol's Factory studio in New York, Jimi Hendrix, Italian architecture groups Archizoom and Superstudio … A field trip to Paris included the Pierre Charreau-designed house and medical suite known as the Maison de Verre (1928–32) and Renzo Piano and Richard Rogers' barge on the River Seine where they worked on the Pompidou Centre. Kelly's first design jobs were sets for two RCA fashion shows, plus the interior for the RCA student 'Art Bar' to which he gave the name. He was at the RCA for three years. During this time he morphed into what the other students called 'the Photo Kid' – gone was the long hair and student garb, replaced by 'brothel-creeper' shoes, fluorescent socks, drainpipe trousers and short cropped hair. When anyone wanted to take a picture of RCA students, they often featured the Photo Kid.

Big Breaks
The early to mid-1970s for Kelly oscillated between the then avant-garde epicentres of Covent Garden (with its Zanzibar night spot) and the King's Road, Chelsea. His first break came when he was asked to design the façade and interior of Covent Garden's HOWIE boutique (1976). This was a fledgling version of what has become Kelly's trademark lexicon of forms, materials and preoccupations – mesh, industrial flooring and partitioning, and in this case an instantly recognisable façade with its diagonal, fractured emphasis.

The diagonal was again to feature in Kelly's façade for 430 King's Road, for Malcolm McLaren and Vivienne Westwood's Seditionaries emporium (1976), commissioned as they were impressed by the HOWIE shop.

It was also during this time that he met Peter Saville.

Metallic Perforated Sleeves
During his last year at the RCA, Kelly had written a thesis influenced by the American writer and artist of the Beat Generation William S Burroughs: it had a metal cover with its title 'METAL LINED CUBICLES – THE PHOTO KID' industrially embossed on it. Saville had shown a particular interest in it whilst visiting Kelly's flat. By very early 1980 the two were working on record cover designs together. The duo's first collaboration was a 1980 cover for the post-punk band Orchestral Manoeuvres in the Dark (OMD) – the album cover was inspired by the metal perforated shop door at HOWIE.

Swiftly after that came the award-winning 12-inch record cover for the self-titled album for the same group, a perforated cover of blue and an inner sleeve of orange. Kelly has always been interested in industrial materials, particularly steels, iron and aluminium. His HOWIE store rejoiced in metallic finishes and perforated-steel flooring patterns. Using the same idea, there were many iterations and colour combinations for subsequent OMD releases and editions.

**Ben Kelly Design,
The Haçienda,
Manchester,
1982**

The interior looking towards the Kim Philby Bar. Kelly's use of the striated hazard-tape marking – here, yellow and black, red and black, and white and black around columns – punctuates the space, contrasting with a cooler bluey-grey.

A little later that year, in April 1980, the Manchester band Joy Division released a single called 'Love Will Tear Us Apart' in a sleeve designed by Kelly and Saville inspired by the metallic cover of Kelly's thesis. 'Love Will Tear Us Apart' was a massive hit for Factory Records and the label decided to create a nightclub that would be a centre of their activities and a hub for a generation of musical exploration. Ben Kelly was asked to design it, converting an old yacht showroom in Central Manchester. Saville had suggested him when approached to design it himself, as Kelly already had experience at an architectural scale.

FAC51

The brief, if it can be called that, was free flowing – a glorified village hall, or a 'cathedral' as Tony Wilson called it. The accommodation consisted of a stage, dance floor, toilets, cloakroom and three bars. The small cocktail bar in the basement was called 'The Gay Traitor' in reference to Anthony Blunt, a British art historian who spied for the Soviets, and the two other bars were named after his fellow spies: the Kim Philby Bar (the main bar) and Hicks (codename of Guy Burgess), a small bar on the balcony. Wilson also had an interest in the French Situationists with their psycho-geographic drifting, the shifting ambience and the surreal magic of cities – which is why The Haçienda's name is inspired by one of their manifestoes, Ivan Chtcheglov's 'Formulary for a New Urbanism', originally written in 1953, which declares 'The haçienda must be built.'[3]

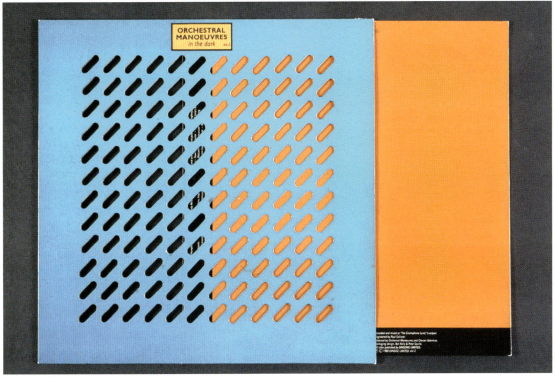

Ben Kelly and Peter Saville, Orchestral Manoeuvres in the Dark album cover, 1980

Taking its lead from the metal perforated door installed at the entrance to the HOWIE store, the sleeve is also perforated, revealing Kelly's trademark orange on the inside dust jacket.

Factory Records' name is obviously a reference to Andy Warhol's Factory art studio in New York (1963–87). Kelly has a great admiration for both Warhol and Marcel Duchamp. Of Warhol he says: 'No one summoned up America at that time in all its powerful aspects more than Warhol.' Duchamp was an enigmatic figure with his ready-made objects, glass drawing/paintings and anamorphic installations. Ben Kelly Design's logo is Duchamp's chocolate grinder from his *Large Glass* (1915–23), digitised in pre-digital days by pulling a drawing of it through a fax machine. It is through a thorough appreciation of these artists that Kelly has honed his working practices, drawing on everyday materiality/codification and the *objet trouvé* (found object).

Everything Factory Records produced had an official designation, and The Haçienda was FAC51. Kelly conceived the venue as a great artwork. It is a festival of colour, industrial aesthetics and everyday symbolism immediately recognisable to its audience and users. Compositionally, The Haçienda reflected the zeitgeist of the day, which had yet to be defined, and this was a huge part of its iconic success. It mixed Deconstructivism with Postmodernism and sparing emphasis on bright colours, all mixed together in Kelly's inimitable style. It was visually beguiling yet highly resilient, so as to accommodate high-energy clubbing. It is a cacophony of black-and-yellow hazard tape, roadside reflective bollards, exposed steel columned trusses supporting the roof, perforated metal panels all punctuated by zones of alternating diagonal colour and lighting rigs. It is not hard to imagine it as a contemporary cathedral – a place of shamanic trance and musical epiphany.

Saving Orange
One day in the early 1980s, Kelly was walking opposite the Victoria and Albert Museum in Kensington when he was stunned to find what he describes as the 'perfect orange', on the hoardings around the building site of the Ismaili Centre, coincidently designed by his old RCA tutor's firm Casson Conder Partnership and built in 1979–85. He enquired what paint it was, and was given an empty tin. When Kelly designed the Smile hair salon in Chelsea's King's Road, which opened in 1984, the magazine *The World of Interiors* opined: 'Ben Kelly rescued the colour orange from the scrap heap of style.'[4] Flashes of that orange permeate The Haçienda and it is his trademark colour.

Virtual Insanity
In keeping with the multispace theme of this issue of ⌀, The Haçienda after its demolition in 1997 has, with the help of London design firm Morph, ascended into the virtual realm. In 2009, two beautiful limited-edition prints were created digitally and offered for sale, one called *Haçienda West* and the other

**Ben Kelly Design,
The FAC51 Haçienda plaque,
1997**

A commemorative plaque placed into the brickwork of the building, now converted into apartments, in which The Haçienda once stood. Note the red, and the cedilla reminiscent of the five in FAC51.

Justin Metz, Brendan Mannion and Ben Kelly,
Screen grab from The Haçienda virtual
fly-through model,
2015–20

What is extraordinary about this model is its attention to detail. Every rivet, every light and its beam, every colour and every material surface is depicted in hyper-realistic exactitude – so every virtual clubber feels they are there. A testament to the skill and technologies we now have at our disposal.

In keeping with the multispace theme of this issue of ⌂, The Haçienda after its demolition in 1997 has, with the help of London design firm Morph, ascended into the virtual realm

Haçienda East. During 2015, Ben Kelly and New Order bassist Peter Hook (who owns the name 'Haçienda') were approached by creative directors Justin Metz and Brendan Mannion about the prospect of constructing a full virtual fly-through model of the club. On New Year's Eve 2020, as a tribute to DJ Frankie Knuckles, his 2013/14 New Year's Eve set was incorporated in a virtual model and broadcast of the club[5] – four million people watched, and an app is currently being developed.

In a demonstration of the cyclic nature of history, book-ending his career, Kelly has recently been commissioned to co-design with design practice Brinkworth the public-facing interiors for a new Manchester music, event and performance venue, Aviva Studios – Factory International (opened October 2023, architect OMA). One imagines orange will figure in it somewhere! ⌂

Notes
1. Ivan Chtcheglov, 'Formulaire pour un urbanisme nouveau', written 1953; full English version, tr Ken Knabb, in *Écrits retrouvés*, Éditions Allia (Paris), 2006: https://www.bopsecrets.org/SI/Chtcheglov.htm.
2. All quotes are from an online interview with Ben Kelly by Neil Spiller, 28 February 2023.
3. Chtcheglov, *op cit*.
4. 'Hair Style', *The World of Interiors*, November 1984: https://www.worldofinteriors.com/story/smile-ben-kelly-1984.
5. Haciendapress, 'Haçienda NYE Tribute to Frankie Knuckles', 27 December 2020: https://www.fac51-thehacienda.com/hacienda-nye-tribute-to-frankie-knuckles/.

Text © 2023 John Wiley & Sons Ltd. Images: pp 128–9, 130–31(t), 132(b) © Ben Kelly Design; p 131(b) © Ben Kelly and Peter Saville; pp 132–33(t) © Ben Kelly, CGI Justin Metz and Brendan Mannion

Joshua Bard is an Associate Professor at the School of Architecture at Carnegie Mellon University in Pittsburgh, Pennsylvania. He is an architectural educator conducting applied research at the intersection of construction culture and robotic technology. His teaching and research interrogate traditional binaries in design culture (industry/craft, machine/hand, virtual/physical space, and digital/analogue production), discovering new potential for contemporary digital tools in the jettisoned logics of hand and material craft. He creates augmented construction and design systems combining the best of human skill, algorithmic translation and robotic automation.

Sasha Belitskaja is an architectural designer and digital artist who pushes the boundaries of traditional design with surrealistic works that explore the intersection of physical and digital spaces. With a background in architecture, she has exhibited her work globally and worked for design and tech companies, creating new products, visual design and interactive content. She received her BArch with distinction from the University of Dundee, Scotland, and her MArch with distinction from the University of Applied Arts Vienna, in Studio Greg Lynn. She has worked for internationally renowned design offices in Stuttgart, Vienna, London and Los Angeles, and is a co-founder of the iheartblob extended-reality architectural design studio.

Alice Bucknell is a North American artist and writer based in London and Los Angeles. Working primarily through game engines and speculative fiction, her work explores interconnections of architecture, ecology, magic, and nonhuman and machine intelligence. In 2021 she founded New Mystics, a digital platform merging magic and technology. She is an Associate Lecturer in MA Narrative Environments at the University of the Arts, London. She is currently a Supercollider SciArt Ambassador in LA, and in residence at transmediale in Berlin. She studied anthropology at the University of Chicago, and Critical Practice at the Royal College of Arts, London.

Ibiye Camp is an artist who engages with technology, trade and materials within the African diaspora. Her work utilises architectural tools to create sound and video, accompanied by augmented reality and 3D objects, and highlights the biases and conflicts inherent to technology and postcolonial subjects. She holds a MArch from the Royal College of Art, and a BA (Hons) in Fine Art from Central Saint Martins, University of the Arts London. She is the co-founder of Xcessive Aesthetics, an interdisciplinary design collective exploring data through immersive technologies and public installations, which also runs the Digital Native BA studio at the Design Academy Eindhoven, the Netherlands. Her work has been exhibited at the Venice Architecture Biennale, Shanghai Biennale, Istanbul Design Biennial, Triennale Milano and the Sharjah Architecture Triennial.

Jesse Damiani is a curator, writer and advisor in new media art and emerging technologies. He is Arts & Culture Advisor for open-source R&D company Protocol Labs, Senior Curator at Nxt Museum in Amsterdam, and the Host of Adobe's Taking Shape, a hub for 3D art and design. An affiliate of the metaLAB (at) Harvard, and the Institute for the Future in Palo Alto, California, his writing has appeared in *Billboard*, *Forbes*, *NBC News*, *The Verge* and *WIRED*. He is the founder of Postreality Labs, a strategic sensemaking studio and consultancy in LA, as well as the *Reality Studies* newsletter.

Wendy W Fok trained as an architect, and is interested in design, technology and creative solutions for the built environment. They have experience in product development and programme management from zero to launch, design-build, manufacturing, hardware/software and digital fabrication. They hold a Doctor of Design from the Harvard University Graduate School of Design (GSD) in Cambridge, Massachusetts, in partnership with the Harvard Law School, obtained a MArch and Certification of Urban Policy/Planning from Princeton University, New Jersey, and a Bachelor of Arts in Architecture with a concentration in Economics (Statistics) from Barnard College, Columbia University, New York.

Fredrik Hellberg is an architect and educator. He has held academic positions at the John H Daniels Faculty of Architecture, Landscape and Design at the University of Toronto, Canada; Architectural Association (AA) School of Architecture, London; and the International Program in Design and Architecture (INDA) at Chulalongkorn University in Bangkok, Thailand. With Lara Lesmes he founded the multidisciplinary design and research practice Space Popular, and together they direct an Advanced Topics studio of the same name at the faculty of Architecture and Urban Design at the University of California, Los Angeles (UCLA). The practice works across the physical and virtual realms, with several built projects and numerous exhibitions in Asia and Europe. They have worked for private clients and public institutions, and exhibited in group shows as well as solo exhibitions.

Andrew Kovacs is a Los Angeles-based architectural designer and educator. His work on architecture and urbanism has been published widely, including in *A+U*, *Pidgin*, *Project*, *Pool*, *Perspecta*, *Manifest*, *Metropolis*, *Clog*, *Domus* and *The Real Review*. He is the creator and curator of the Archive of Affinities website devoted to the collection and display of architectural b-sides. In 2015 he published the book, *Architectural Affinities* as part of the Treatise series organised and sponsored by the Graham Foundation in Chicago. His design studio, Office Kovacs, works on projects at all scales. Recent work includes a proposal for a network of parks in the downtown Los Angeles alleys, a large-scale installation entitled *Colossal Cacti* at the Coachella Valley Music and Arts Festival, and an experimental camping pavilion in the Morongo Valley desert in Southern California.

Lara Lesmes
Lara Lesmes is an architectural designer and educator. She has held academic positions at the John H Daniels Faculty of Architecture, Landscape and Design at the University of Toronto; AA School of Architecture, and INDA at Chulalongkorn University, Bangkok.

CONTRIBUTORS

She is the co-founder, with Fredrik Hellberg, of multidisciplinary design and research practice and studio Space Popular. The practice's work has featured in exhibitions at the Swedish Centre for Architecture and Design (ArkDes) in Stockholm; Gallery Magazin, Vienna; the Royal Institute of British Architects (RIBA) and Sir John Soane's Museum, London; MAXXI – National Museum of 21st Century Art, Rome; and the Museum of Applied Arts (MAK), Vienna.

Micaela Mantegna is a scholar and activist, specialising in artificial intelligence and extended reality ethics, video-game law and metaverse governance. Currently a TED Fellow, an affiliate at the Berkman Klein Center at Harvard University, and a member of the Future Council of the Metaverse at the World Economic Forum, her work has been featured globally in publications including *WIRED*, *The Verge* and *Le Monde*. Her first book, *ARTficial: Creativity, Artificial Intelligence and Copyright*, was published in 2022.

Holly Nielsen is a historian, writer and narrative designer based in London. She is currently completing her PhD at Royal Holloway, University of London. Her thesis is titled 'British Board Games and the Ludic Imagination, *c* 1860–1960'. Before pivoting to academia and games, she was a journalist and arts critic, writing for *The Guardian*, *The New Statesman* and *Vice*, among others.

Giacomo Pala is an architect, designer and scholar. He works as a research associate at the Institute of Architectural Theory at the Faculty of Architecture at the University of Innsbruck, Austria, where he investigates the concept of syncretism theoretically and historically, as well as through teaching design workshops, projects and exhibitions. He has previously held workshops at various institutions, including Chulalongkorn University in Bangkok, collaborated with various studios, and tested his hypotheses through projects, publications, book chapters, installations and exhibitions in Vienna, Venice, Innsbruck, Vezprem and elsewhere.

Marcelo Rinesi is an AI architecture and strategy consultant. He is Chief AI Architect for Axenya in São Paulo, Brazil, and consults with companies, NGOs, journalists, and other civil society actors on how to adapt to and leverage emerging cognitive technologies, as well as being Chief Technology Officer of the Institute for Ethics and Emerging Technologies technoprogressive think tank. He also publishes the short sci-fi newsletter *Adversarial Metanoia*.

Neil Spiller is Editor of *D*, and was previously Hawksmoor Chair of Architecture and Landscape and Deputy Pro Vice Chancellor at the University of Greenwich in London. Prior to this he was Vice Dean at the Bartlett School of Architecture, University College London (UCL). He has made an international reputation as an architect, designer, artist, teacher, writer and polemicist. He is the founding director of the Advanced Virtual and Technological Architecture Research (AVATAR) group, which continues to push the boundaries of architectural design and discourse in the face of the impact of 21st-century technologies. Its current preoccupations include augmented and mixed realities and other metamorphic technologies.

Paula Strunden is a transdisciplinary artist with a background in architecture. She studied in Vienna, Paris and London, and worked at Raumlabor Berlin and Herzog & de Meuron Basel. Since 2020, she has been conducting her PhD at the Academy of Fine Arts Vienna as part of the European network Communities of Tacit Knowledge: Architecture and its Ways of Knowing (TACK). Her extended-reality installations have been exhibited internationally, and were nominated for the Dutch Film Award 'Gouden Calf' (in 2020 and 2023). As Associate of London-based collective Store, and co-founder of educational initiative Virtual Fruits, she teaches extended-reality courses and workshops, and advocates for an alternative historiography of virtual technologies through her platform www.xr-atlas.org.

Lucia Tahan is an architect based in Los Angeles. She specialises in spatial computing and has produced buildings, installations, augmented reality and software. Her work was exhibited at the Venice Architecture Biennale in 2023 and 2018, and at venues such as MAXXI in Rome, the Seoul Architecture Biennale and Lisbon Architecture Triennale.

Francesca Torello is an architectural historian and is Special Faculty with the School of Architecture at Carnegie Mellon University. She writes about the role of history in architectural education and practice, particularly at the turn of the 20th century. She reflects on the shifts digital technologies produce in long-standing cultural institutions, such as museums and archives. Her research explores architecture's mediatic power, the selective histories buildings convey and how they operate as pedagogical spaces.

Liam Young is a designer, director and BAFTA-nominated producer who operates in the spaces between design, fiction and futures. His visionary films and speculative worlds are both extraordinary images of tomorrow and urgent examinations of the environmental questions facing us today. As a worldbuilder, he visualises the cities, spaces and props of our imaginary futures for the film and television industry. His films have been shown on platforms such as the BBC, Venice Biennale and Royal Academy of Arts, collected by cultural organisations such as the Museum of Modern Art (MoMA), New York, Art Institute of Chicago, Victoria and Albert Museum, London, National Gallery of Victoria and M Plus, Hong Kong, and featured in *WIRED*, *New Scientist*, *Arte*, *Canal+*, *Time* magazine and many more.

What is *Architectural Design*?

Founded in 1930, *Architectural Design* (△) is an influential and prestigious publication. It combines the currency and topicality of a newsstand journal with the rigour and production qualities of a book. With an almost unrivalled reputation worldwide, it is consistently at the forefront of cultural thought and design.

Issues of △ are edited either by the journal Editor, Neil Spiller, or by an invited Guest-Editor. Renowned for being at the leading edge of design and new technologies, △ also covers themes as diverse as architectural history, the environment, interior design, landscape architecture and urban design.

Provocative and pioneering, △ inspires theoretical, creative and technological advances. It questions the outcome of technical innovations as well as the far-reaching social, cultural and environmental challenges that present themselves today.

For further information on △, subscriptions and purchasing single issues see:

https://onlinelibrary.wiley.com/journal/15542769

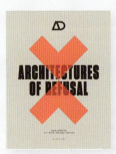

Volume 92 No 6
ISBN 978-1-119-83396-3

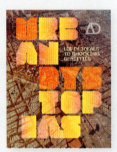

Volume 93 No 1
ISBN 978-1-119-83399-4

Volume 93 No 2
ISBN 978-1-119-83835-7

Volume 93 No 3
ISBN 978-1-119-83442-7

Volume 93 No 2
ISBN 978-1-119-98396-5

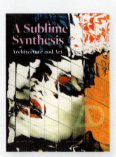

Volume 93 No 2
ISBN 978-1-394-17079-1

Individual backlist issues of △ are available as books for purchase starting at £29.99 / US$45.00

wiley.com

How to Subscribe
With 6 issues a year, you can subscribe to △ either print or online.

https://onlinelibrary.wiley.com/journal/15542769

Institutional subscription
£357 / US$666
online only

£373 / US$695
print only

£401 / US$748
print and online

Personal-rate subscription
£151 / US$236
print only

Student-rate subscription
£97 / US$151
print only

Individual issue:
£9.99 / US$13.99

To subscribe to print or online
E: cs-journals@wiley.com
W: https://onlinelibrary.wiley.com/journal/15542769

Americas
E: cs-journals@wiley.com
T: +1 877 762 2974

Europe, Middle East and Africa
E: cs-journals@wiley.com
T: +44 (0)18 6577 8315

Asia Pacific
E: cs-journals@wiley.com
T: +65 6511 8000

Japan (for Japanese-speaking support)
E: cs-japan@wiley.com
T: +65 6511 8010

Visit our Online Customer Help
available in 7 languages at www.wileycustomerhelp.com/ask